It's About Relationships

It's About Relationships

How to Fix Broken Relationships

Dorothea Johnson James

Xulon Press

Xulon Press
555 Winderley Pl, Suite 225
Maitland, FL 32751
407.339.4217
www.xulonpress.com

© 2024 by Dorothea Johnson James

All rights reserved solely by the author. The author guarantees all contents are original and do not infringe upon the legal rights of any other person or work. No part of this book may be reproduced in any form without the permission of the author.

Due to the changing nature of the Internet, if there are any web addresses, links, or URLs included in this manuscript, these may have been altered and may no longer be accessible. The views and opinions shared in this book belong solely to the author and do not necessarily reflect those of the publisher. The publisher therefore disclaims responsibility for the views or opinions expressed within the work.

Unless otherwise indicated, Scripture quotations taken from the New Revised Standard Version (NRSV). Copyright © 1989 the Division of Christian Education of the National Council of the Churches of Christ in the United States of America.

Paperback ISBN-13: 979-8-86850-111-1
Ebook ISBN-13: 979-8-86850-112-8

Table of Contents

Acknowledgements................................ vii

Dedication...................................... ix

Introduction xiii

1. The Process of Reconciliation and Relationships . . . 1

2. We Have to Start Somewhere.................... 19

3. There Is a Method to the Madness 87

4. Summing it all Up 139

About the Author................................ 141

Bibliography 145

Acknowledgements

IN CONSIDERING EXPRESSIONS of thanks and appreciation on paper, sharing the poem "With Gratitude" seemed appropriate:

> You, said, 'Call us, any time you need us,' and I felt at home in your words. I poured out my grief, and you hugged me. I told you my fears, and you prayed that I would sleep protected. I expressed my confusion, and you helped me sort out the parts. I tried to face my ugly self, and you kept on caring. I gave you my pain and you gave me a kiss. How can I say thank you? How do I express this awareness that I have found a home in your love?[1]

If you ever have been encouraged by me or have imprinted on my life in any way, I am grateful.

---

[1] Marva J. Dawn, *Truly the Community: Romans 12 and How to Be the Church* (Grand Rapids, MI: William B. Eerdmans Publishing Company, 1998), 215.

Dedication

A SPECIAL DEDICATION to my dear and beloved mother, Georgia Johnson, and my grandmother, Viva Johnson, for investing in my life.

> When I understand my enemy well enough to defeat him, then in that moment, I also love him.
> –A. E. Wiggins

Introduction

I AM REMINDED of a very old riddle that Mother Goose turned into a nursery rhyme. From our childhood, we can recite the words:

> *Humpty Dumpty sat on a wall,*
> *Humpty Dumpty had a great fall.*
> *All the King's horses and all the King's men*
> *Couldn't put Humpty together again!*[2]

Many of us often discover ourselves entangled in fractured relationships that seem beyond repair. This book is tailored to reach out to individuals grappling with issues of disconnection, exacerbated by communication barriers and the sheer frustration that can arise within relationships. Its purpose is to offer valuable guidance and instruction grounded in biblical principles to those who may, at times, feel either unwilling or unable to mend these fractured relationships.

---

[2] The Poetry Foundation, *Mother Goose Nursery Rhymes, Humpty Dumpty Sat on A Wall* (Chicago, IL: Harriet Monroe Poetry Institute, 2014), http://www.poetryfoundation.org/poem/176327 (accessed May 9, 2014).

It's About Relationships

In this tumultuous world, relationships often become intricate and painful. Below are several poignant statements from individuals who might resonate with the plight of Humpty Dumpty:

- "I had heard you were in town this weekend, so I dressed up and waited for the doorbell to ring. You never showed up. Maybe you'll return on Father's Day."
- "I placed my trust in you. You brought me gifts and spoke kindly, but then you hurt me. I suppose that's just what uncles do."
- "I may be different from most people, but does that justify the negativity? Why do you talk about me, ignore me, and attempt to undermine me? Is it because I'm simply not like you?"
- "I am your child—warm, loving, and intelligent. Why do you tell people I was a mistake?"
- "Just because I share their name doesn't mean I'll grow up to be exactly like them."
- "We argue incessantly. You wound me, and I retaliate. Yet, for the sake of our children and to ward off embarrassment, we remain together."
- "At times, you exude insecurity, display untrustworthiness, and lack integrity. Still, I portray you as a diamond to the world and advocate for your cause. Do you care? Not in the least. It's precisely what you expect of me, nothing more, nothing less."

Introduction

- "Friends, how many of us truly have them? That's the real question. Why are you only my friend when you need something from me?"
- "Sticks and stones may break my bones, but words can indeed hurt me. What you said hurt, and it was intentional. As a result, you've been unfriended."
- "I did everything in my power to keep you and make you love me. In the process, I lost the most valuable thing I had—myself."
- "I comprehend that you couldn't be responsible for me twenty-four hours a day. But could you spare a minute or two to let me know you love me nonetheless?"
- "It's ironic how you never have time for the things I ask you to do, yet exerting effort and using kind words aren't an issue when it comes to other people."
- "So, you kept me close because you didn't want me to discover you had someone else. Was I truly that naive, or were my standards that low from the beginning?"
- "I keep convincing myself that I'm better off without anyone, mainly because I don't think anyone desires me."
- "The toll I pay for trying to meet your expectations: my sanity, my self-esteem, my aspirations, and my dreams. Why continue living?"

It's About Relationships

Indeed, everyone is born into a biological family with the natural expectation of being nurtured and loved. Regrettably, the myriad twists and turns of life frequently erect barriers of indifference, anger, and apathy toward both family members and friends. In the book *The Lord Will Provide*, the author deals with conflict and says, "We all know that conflict is a way of life. We cannot avoid conflict. We can't shun disagreements. We can't stay away from disputes."[3] As we grow and reach an age of understanding, it becomes almost inevitable that we will encounter some form of conflict. Conflict is an inherent part of life, and the challenge lies in how we navigate these conflicts and preserve our relationships with others. Often, we find ourselves ill-equipped to mend the rifts in relationships that result from these conflicts, disputes, and disagreements.

When faced with conflict, many people adopt the mindset of "I can manage on my own" or "I don't need them anyway" instead of seeking resolution. However, the truth is that we are created by a benevolent and compassionate God who desires harmony among us. Relationships are the cornerstone of human existence.

Dr. P. M. Smith, the pastor of Huber Memorial Baptist Church in Baltimore, Maryland, wisely states, "If it is not about relationships, it is not about nothin'." The essence of this statement is that we must constantly strive to improve our relationships. Unfortunately, we cannot achieve this in

---

[3] Lucius M. Dalton, *The Lord Will Provide* (Bloomington, IN: Author House, 2011), 20.

isolation. We require God's guidance because maintaining relationships is a complex and challenging endeavor.

The world is marred by brokenness, with the presence of sin acting as a significant obstacle to maintaining productive, loving, and supportive relationships. Conquering life's manifold challenges necessitates the preservation of healthy relationships, which, in turn, hinges on the practices of reconciliation, seeking God's presence, and active engagement within the community of believers. This book will elucidate these three fundamental principles by drawing insights from the spiritual disciplines outlined in Genesis 50 and Acts 2.

As human beings, we should inherently engage in the process of reconciling relationships. When we find ourselves in an environment that permits us to acknowledge the fractures and apply the tenets of spiritual disciplines, the healing and restoration of relationships become attainable. Thus, when Humpty Dumpty falls from the relationship wall, feeling shattered and bruised, he need not rely on all the king's horses or all the king's men. Instead, he should turn to God and the teachings of the Word of God, for it is there that he can discover the path to restoration.

> *"Here comes that dreamer!" they said to each other. "Come now, let's kill him and throw him into one of these cisterns and say that a ferocious animal devoured him. Then we'll see what comes of his dreams."*[4]

---

[4] Genesis 50:19-20 (Revised Standard Version).

Joseph's brothers allowed their feelings and emotions to guide their actions. It's important to recognize that feelings and emotions are genuine and demand appropriate attention. Situations like these can become significant obstacles to the growth of relationships, both within the family and the Church. Reconciliation becomes a formidable challenge when we neglect to engage in the specific spiritual disciplines, such as immersing ourselves in the teachings of the apostles, partaking in the act of breaking bread (Holy Communion), fostering fellowship, and maintaining a continuous life of prayer.

The mindset of "every man for himself" and "I can succeed all by myself" has infiltrated the Church, eroding the sense of community, love, and forgiveness. This phenomenon appears to be particularly pronounced in every ethnic and culturally different communities.

In his book *New Wine, New Wineskins*, F. Douglas Powe, Jr., says that "It is important to understand the cultural shifts within the African American community because it will give us new insights on how congregations will have to think differently"[5] when he talks about how we do ministry. The mindset of the churchgoer has shifted over time. In today's church, many newcomers have little to no prior experience with church principles and the timeless wisdom imparted by our grandparents. Understanding

---

[5] F. Douglas Powe, Jr., *New Wine, New Wineskins: How African American Congregations Can Reach New Generations* (Nashville: Abingdon Press, 2012), 2.

the importance of forgiveness, the empowerment of concealing the Word in one's heart, and the effectiveness of prayer through faith is not the same as consistently putting these principles into practice with unwavering dedication. Merely adopting the belief that "all is well that ends well" could result in an assembly of individuals who seem lifeless and are ill-prepared to respond when called upon to make a meaningful impact. If the community of believers continues down this path, it runs the risk of becoming a group of insincere, self-absorbed individuals who have disconnected themselves from the true source of power. This is why I firmly believe that we must revisit the fundamentals and draw inspiration from the model set by the initial community of believers. They were also new to this way of life, and it proved to be effective for them.

When individuals fail to acknowledge their own brokenness, they often find themselves trapped in a cycle of hardship and despair. The family unit stands as one of the most influential and observable models in the world. In its intended form, it should exemplify God's love for His children. Similar to a mirror's reflection, people should witness in the Church the love, care, and genuine concern for each other's well-being, which should draw them closer to God. Both the family and the Church should serve as places of refuge, guided growth, and joyous victories. The strength we gain from functional family units and thriving church communities equips us to conquer even the most daunting mountains and endure the darkest valleys. Those fortunate enough to possess these familial connections have achieved remarkable positive strides in life. In his book, *Organic Church,* Neil Cole discusses the significance of having as little as two or three in the group, and how that intimate closeness makes community, accountability, confidentiality, and flexibility stronger.[6] The Church embodies the same idea of a tightly-knit unit, one that is proximate enough to reach out and touch, comprehend, provide solace, love, and support, and, if required, rescue. Conversely, individuals lacking an understanding of this functional unity have consistently faced obstacles and struggled to demonstrate their true potential to the world.

This model will bring to light what appears to be an evidentiary dilemma within many family units that are broken. It is more and more common to see abuse, disputes, hatred, and indifference in the family unit. These negative values persist to destroy the community concept, and even appears to be normal at times. One of the most prevalent sayings in our society is "we are all dysfunctional, so why complain or look for brighter days." It appears that societies, and even the government, have failed to respond to this important and significant predicament. The result of this ignorance can be detrimental to everyone involved. In his book, *Growing True Disciples*, George Barna said, "It is inadequate to simply fill people's heads with Bible verses

---

[6] Neil Cole, *Organic Church: Growing Faith Where Life Happens* (San Francisco, CA: Jossey Bass, 2005), 101.

and principles."[7] There is more to Christianity than just individual learning. Growing in the family of God requires interacting with family life. Locally and universally, the Church should be the family model as well as reflect the family model. In its current state, many families do not represent the love, mercy, or grace that God intended. However, as we learn, apply, and model these principles in our Christian communities, we begin to model these principles in our homes and eventually in the entire world.

The heart of the writer is to show there are many individuals who have been unable to find the necessary guidance, compassion, and growth they need to properly mature. Our sons and daughters are on the battlefield without back up. Where there is no guidance and no structure, there is a lack of growth and rules, and anything goes. A disciple-making community can be a great vehicle to reintroduce individuals to the wholeness God intends.

Individually, we may be dysfunctional or have some broken pieces. However, when we place our broken vessels in the hand of the Master, restoration is available. When we learn and practice the ways of God, dysfunctional becomes functional. It is time to pick ourselves up and dust ourselves off. Humpty Dumpty could not do it because he placed his trust in the king's horses and the king's men, but we will put our trust in the Son of The Living God. The Potter of the human race is ready to put

---

[7] George Barna, *Growing True Disciples* (Colorado Springs, CO: Water Brook Press, 2001), 89.

us back together again. Through the process of applying the disciplines of the Church, we are able to model the costly grace to our families.

According to Dietrich Bonhoeffer, costly grace is one that requires us to follow and submit to Jesus Christ.[8] Submission is not always the way we want it to be. Submission is not always without pain. In godly submission, we rest in the love and mercy of God and just like an experienced carpenter, we begin to rebuild houses from the inside out.

In summation, the world is in desperate need of redirection and rejuvenation. If our attitudes of selfishness or oneness continues, the result will adversely affect the future of the entire world. This book will present a proposal in which the Church serves as the catalyst for bringing relationships back in line with God's timeless principles. Neil Anderson indicates that "fulfillment as a Christian is based on understanding who you are—specifically your identity in Christ as a child of God."[9] The Church will serve as the change agent first for the individual and then for the entire church family. It is love and care for individual concerns that makes us open to grow in the Word of God. Merciful forgiveness helps us to embrace the importance of submitting and serving God. Lastly, it

---

[8] Dietrich Bonheoffer, *The Cost of Discipleship* (Nashville: Broadman and Holman Publishers, 1998), 45.

[9] Neil Anderson, *Victory Over the Darkness* (Ventura: Regal Books, 1990), 18.

is the testimony of grace applied to our lives that helps others see the loving kindness of God. If the Church fails to model true relationships and continues to ignore the broken people directly in its reach, it will have failed to represent the sacrificial love of God.

"It's better to resolve a conflict than to dissolve a relationship." – Josh McDowell

Chapter One

The Process of Reconciliation and Relationships

So, what is this all about? I've spent a lifetime wondering how to fix my family. I have always wanted loving brothers and sisters, caring and nurturing parents, grandparents, aunties and uncles, and cousins who had my back. You know the kind that will fight you and fight for you. The kind that shows up when you need them, and who know you better than you know yourself. So, before you judge me by talking about my peeps. Let me say I believe my family did the best they could with what they had to work with in this world, and I love them. Unfortunately, we have not achieved that much wanted relationship. I'll say it although they may never say it. All of us are broken, just like Humpty Dumpty.

Larry Crab, a prominent psychologist and biblical teacher, penned a book entitled *Connecting: Healing for Ourselves and Our Relationships.* In this book, he articulates the concept that community has the "potential to liberate, strengthen, and encourage […] a few and to touch the deepest, deadest, most terrifying parts of [...] people's souls with resurrection power."[10] Small groups and family circles have the potential to be healing communities. "The greatest need in modern civilization is the development of communities—true communities are where the heart of God is, where the humble and wise learn to shepherd those on the path behind them, where trusting stragglers lock arms with others as together they journey on."[11] Crabb wants his readers to come away knowing we are not in this world alone and there is power in genuine relationships. He provides the three ingredients of an effective healing community.

> Relationships heal when they reflect the energy of Christ. We can impact others by: Letting people know we delight in them as Christ does; Eagerly looking for the goodness in someone's heart and identifying the passions that are promoting loving, strong choices; and exposing the darkness in someone's heart, their sin and pain, in order to engage them more convincingly with the Savior's kindness; it's the kindness of God that leads to repentance.[12]

---

[10] Larry Crabb, *Connecting: Healing for Ourselves and Our Relationships a Radical New Vision* (Nashville, TN: Word Publishing, 1997), xv.

[11] Ibid., xvii.

[12] Ibid., 21.

The Process of Reconciliation and Relationships

This formula should be effective because, according to Crabb, individuals are designed to connect. Therefore, our failure to make a connection with others hinders our effectiveness.

Robert L. Browning and Roy Reed's book, *Forgiveness, Reconciliation, and Moral Courage*, examines and explores the Church's message of forgiveness, reconciliation, and its power to heal. According to their survey of churches, the largest number of respondents chose to define sin as a failure of love, specifically, the failure to love God and the neighbor.[13] How do we tap into that kind of love? Love that never gives up. We have that kind of love in our grasp. We just have to seize it.

We have to embody forgiveness as Gregory Jones speaks of when he proposes that forgiveness is "not so much a word spoken, and action performed, or a feeling felt as it is an embodied way of life in ever-deepening friendship with the Triune God and with others."[14] The ability to exercise forgiveness is part of an ongoing shaping and transitioning relationship. He goes on to say that the Christian account of forgiveness should not focus on the absolution of one's guilt, but on the reconciliation of brokenness, the restoration of communion with God and with

---

[13] Robert L. Browning and Roy A. Reed, *Forgiveness, Reconciliation, and Moral Courage: Motives and Designs from Ministry in a Troubled World* (Grand Rapids, MI: William B. Eerdmans Publishing Company, 2004), 41.

[14] L. Gregory Jones, *Embodying Forgiveness: A Theological Analysis* (Grand Rapids, MI: William B. Eerdmans Publishing Company, 1995), xii.

one another. This is accomplished through the help of the Holy Spirit, the erasing of learned habits, and the gaining of new practices.

Jones follows the thought of the great Dietrich Bonhoeffer and proclaims there is a cost of forgiveness. For the believer, Jesus has already paid it all. He does not want his reader to trivialize forgiveness through modern thinking. He indicates, "Practices and understandings of forgiveness have been undermined and marginalized in contemporary thought and life."[15]

It is important to grasp the concept that forgiveness is not a one-time event in our lives. Jones states:

> Forgiveness is a habit that must be practiced over time within the disciples of the Christian community. This is so because, as I have been suggesting, in the face of sin and evil, God's love moves toward reconciliation by means of forgiveness. Forgiveness aims to restore communion on the part of humans with God, with one another, and with the whole creation. This forgiveness is costly since it involves acknowledging and experiencing the painful truth of human sin and evil at its worst. In the midst of such brokenness, God's forgiveness aims at

---

[15] Ibid., 37.

> healing people's lives and re-creating communion in God's eschatological Kingdom.[16]

Jones has brought to light the whole sense of community and the need to practice spiritual disciplines in order to maintain true forgiveness within the body of believers.

Moving forward, it is evident that, throughout history, men and women of faith were afforded the opportunity to practice the various disciplines of God. The Church presented an opportunity to be in a specific community of people with like understanding and like passions. They are in the same location for reconciliation, worshipping, praying, fellowshipping, and sitting under the instruction of the Word of God. In that fashion, the practices moved from the temple to the home and from church to the home. Given an opportunity to repent and ask for forgiveness, the believer can become reconciled to God and to others.

In his book, *Family Matters*, Victor J. Grigsby proposes that every family has a job to do to ensure unity and connectivity. The writer feels the family has to utilize prayer to help them through the many crises in life. "Prayer is the family anchor. Prayer is the family fastener. Prayer is the clasp to which all other family activity is affixed."[17] In his acronym F.A.M.I.L.Y., the first word represented by the letter "F" is forgiveness. In defining what he means

---

[16] Ibid., 163.

[17] Victor J. Grigsby, *Family Matters: A Guide for Building Godly Homes* (New Brighton, PA: Penn Eagle Publishing, 2010), 42.

by forgiveness, he basically indicates there are no perfect people, no perfect families, no matter how hard we strive for perfection. Therefore, making the need for forgiveness is essential in our relationships.

Forgiveness is an important discipline, and it is intended to be practiced and maintained on a daily basis. In order to live in forgiveness, there must be some the core spiritual disciplines that are the Bible study, prayer, fellowship, sharing in community, service, and worship or celebration. The prevalent discovery concerning forgiveness, reconciliation, and relationship is that they go hand and hand. Individual relationships, and family units possess the healing properties of reconciliation and forgiveness. However, they must be exercised in the space of loving communities. I repeat forgiveness can be achieved at a cost and must be practiced daily. The core of spiritual discipline emphasizes right relationships. The premise that, is if there is a right relationship with God who is Love who is our Creator, then we are able to achieve right relationships with each other.

More on Spiritual Disciplines

The Bible outlines various disciplines for the believer. The word "discipline" is understood as "learning that molds character and enforces correct behavior; from a Latin word meaning 'instruction' or 'training'." To discipline a person or a group means "to put them in a state of good order so that they function in the way intended."[18] For the most part, "In Christian Spirituality, a discipline is a rule of life, or a set pattern of living intended to facilitate spiritual growth and Christian community. Spiritual disciplines are concerned with our lifestyle or our practice of faith and faithful living."[19] It is important to note that, "spiritual disciplines involve more than just psychological change. Their concern is total and complete graced transformation and healing."[20]

In his book, *Celebration of Discipline: The Pathway to Spiritual Growth*, Richard Foster provides an in-depth study of the disciplines of the Church. Foster speaks of his own life experiences where he felt like he was in a desert dry place and unable to pour out to his congregation. He says, "I had no substance, no depth. The people were starving for a word from God, and I had nothing to give them."[21] After researching the subject, Foster tapped into the spiritual well that quenched the thirst of many church fathers and theologians. Foster identified the spiritual disciplines as the door to liberation, indicating they are "best exercised in the midst of our relationships with our husband or wife,

---

[18] Walter A. Elwell, and B. J. Beitzel, *Baker Encyclopedia of the Bible* (Grand Rapids, MI: Baker Book House, 1998), s. v. "Discipline," 631.

[19] Keith Beasley-Topliffe, *The Upper Room Dictionary of Christian Spiritual Formation* (Nashville, TN; Upper Room Books, 2003), 84.

[20] Ibid., 85.

[21] Richard J. Foster, *Celebration of Discipline: The Path to Spiritual Growth, 20th ed.* (San Francisco, CA: Harper Collins Publisher, 1998), xiii.

our brothers and sisters, or our friends and neighbors."[22] Thus, he presents a formula that requires community in the application of the spiritual disciplines.

Foster utilizes the thought process of the apostle Paul, who revealed in the book of Romans that "sin is a condition that plagues the human race."[23] We face many attacks and life circumstances that may cause us to be separated from God and separated from our friends and family. Foster says, "As long as we think we can save ourselves by our own will power, we will only make the evil in us, stronger than ever."[24] When we practice spiritual disciplines, it allows God to work on our sin-sick souls. Foster goes on to build a premise that God has provided disciplines to position us for transformation, blessings, and spiritual growth. When we exercise the spiritual disciplines, we are afforded the opportunity to focus on the betterment of self.

The apostolic church of today provides an excellent example of the multifaceted expression of the spiritual discipline of fellowship. Fellowship in the Greek is *koinōnía* and is identified as the communion or common faith, experiences, and expressions shared by the family of believers as well as the intimate relationship they have

---

[22] Ibid., 1.

[23] Ibid., 4.

[24] Ibid., 5.

with God.[25] Let us delve deeper into the various aspects of Koinonia.

1. Biblical Origins: Koinonia is rooted in the New Testament, particularly in the writings of the apostle Paul and the Acts of the Apostles. In the Greek, koinonia signifies not just simple fellowship but a deep, spiritual communion. It reflects the shared experiences, resources, and values that bind a community of believers together. This idea is often conveyed through passages like Acts 2:42, which describes the early Christian community as devoted to "the fellowship" (koinonia).
2. Communion and Common Faith: Koinonia emphasizes the communal aspect of faith. It involves a shared belief in the teachings and salvation of Jesus Christ. Believers come together in this faith, breaking bread, and sharing in the Eucharist as a profound act of unity and remembrance.
3. Spiritual Intimacy: Koinonia also refers to the intimacy of the relationship believers have with God. It goes beyond a superficial association and calls for a deep, personal connection with the divine. This spiritual intimacy fosters a sense of oneness with God and, in turn, with fellow believers.

---

[25] A. C. Myers, *Eerdmans Bible Dictionary* (Grand Rapids, MI: William B. Eerdmans Publishing Company, 1987), s. v. "Fellowship," 380.

4. Community and Relationships: Koinonia highlights the importance of Christian community. When believers come together, they share not only their faith but also their lives. It's a space where people can let their guard down, be vulnerable, and develop authentic relationships. This fosters an atmosphere of trust and support, where individuals can grow and mature in their faith.
5. Growth of Love: Spending time together in Koinonia deepens the love among believers. This love is not just a casual affection but a selfless, sacrificial love (agape) that reflects the love of Christ. In this context, Koinonia becomes a conduit for expressing and cultivating this love in a tangible way.
6. Service and Sharing: Koinonia is not limited to emotional or spiritual connection. It also involves practical expressions of care and support for one another. Believers are encouraged to share resources, meet each other's needs, and serve one another, reflecting the idea of a caring and compassionate community.
7. Mission and Outreach: Koinonia extends beyond the walls of church. It compels believers to reach out to the broader community and engage in acts of kindness, service, and evangelism. It's a call to extend the love and fellowship experienced within the community to the world.

In summary, Koinonia is a central concept in Christian theology that emphasizes the deep and multifaceted nature of fellowship, communal faith, spiritual intimacy, and love among believers. Without it, we are not fully engaging with the teachings of the Church. It goes beyond mere social interaction and encourages a profound connection with God and one another, resulting in a loving and caring community that seeks to share the message of Christ with the world.

As we continue in the conversation on spiritual disciples, we share a couple other theologians who have pondered on the subject.

1. In his book, *Spiritual Disciplines: A Believer's Openings to the Grace of God* , James Massey says, "Christian growth and development require discipline,"[26] and though we dread the Word of God, it is necessary. According to Massey, discipline helps us to have proper direction; it helps us to change; it permits us to invest our freedom; it provides us controlled responses "by acting responsibly, and productively."[27] Massey discusses the disciplines of meditation–prayer, fasting, dialogue, and worship. He asserts that while "in meditation we seek to discover

---

[26] James Earl Massey, *Spiritual Disciplines,* Third ed. (Anderson, IN: Warner Press, 1985), 2.

[27] Ibid., 21.

and find; in prayer we seek to give and bestow."[28] The change is made possible based on the premise that the discipline of meditation-prayer, being in the presence of God, demands time and forces self-examination.

2. In *The Spirit of the Disciplines: Understanding How God Changes Lives*, Dallas Willard would like his readers to know, "The spirit of the disciplines is nothing but the love of Jesus," and we must take them seriously.[29] The concepts of preparation and sacrifice are evident in this literary piece. Willard explains that success in life lends largely to the extent of our preparation of mind and body. "A baseball player who expects to excel in the game without adequate exercise of his body is no more ridiculous than the Christian who hopes to be able to act in the manner of Christ when put to the test without the appropriate exercise in godly living."[30] His argument is that we must be well versed in spiritual disciplines as well as practice them daily to walk in the manner we are called. However, the practice of spiritual disciplines is no walk in the park. This practice requires, "The intelligent, informed, unyielding resolve to

---

[28] Ibid., 41.

[29] Dallas Willard, *The Spirit of the Disciplines: Understanding How God Changes Lives* (San Francisco, CA: Harper Collins Publishers, 1988), xii.

[30] Ibid., 4.

live as Jesus lived in all aspects of his life, not just in the moment of specific choice or action."[31]

3. Adele Calhoun presents an exhaustive work on the explanation and use of spiritual disciplines. The disciplines, according to Calhoun, allow for transformation and "introduce people to the myriad of ways they could make space in their lives for God."[32] Calhoun list approximately sixty-eight disciplines and desires as an indication that we all should come to understand the desires in our life that God has brought forth. When the desires are prevalent, "transformation happens as you keep company with Jesus."[33] Calhoun contends that spiritual disciplines opens us to God, and can be achieved through the use of the following tools: "Worship God, Open myself to God, Relinquish the false self and idols of my heart, Share my life with others, Hear the word of God, Incarnate Christ's love for the world, and Pray to God [W.O.R.S.H.I.P]."[34] The acronym helps the reader to focus on connecting with God.

---

[31] Ibid., 10

[32] Adele Ahlberg Calhoun, *Spiritual Disciplines Handbook: Practices That Transform Us* (Downers Grove, IL: Inter Varsity Press Books, 2005), 9.

[33] Ibid., 15.

[34] Ibid., 21.

4. In his book *Spiritual Formation as if the Church Mattered: Growing in Christ through Community*, James Wilhoit looks at how the Church appears to have abandoned its main job, which is making disciples through the practice of spiritual formation. The book looks at the old way and provides direction for developing new ways to reach the masses. The book outlines four pillars of formation, including receiving or being open to God's grace, remembering or understanding who we are and why we were created, responding in service to neighbors and the world, and building relationships in the context of community.

5. In his book, *Inner Growth Outer Change*, John H. Westerhoff III speaks to the spiritual disciplines of prayer, community, and the application of the Word. Westerhoff states, "Christian prayer enables us to engage in the Christian spiritual life. It unites piety (our experience of a relationship with God) with politics (our prophetic active relationships with our neighbors and the world)."[35] John Alsup, in his exegetical document of Acts 41:47, indicates there are four chief elements of the early church life: "the instruction of the apostles [the *didache*, catechesis]; *koinonia*; the breaking of bread;

---

[35] John H. Westerhoff III, *Inner Growth Outer Changes: An Educational Guide to Church Renewal* (New York, NY: Seabury Press, 1979), 28.

and prayer [including songs of praise]."[36] It is also noted that the African American Church is now an essential part of the family and the urban community.

6. Donald S. Whitney, a pastor and professor, prepared a work directly related to spiritual disciplines for the Christian life within the Church. In his book, *Spiritual Disciplines for the Christian Life,* he stresses studying the Bible, prayer, worship, evangelism, serving, stewardship, fasting, silence and solitude, journaling, and learning as spiritual disciplines. Whitney speaks to the need to be connected to a body of believers and not be engaged "in a privatized Christianity,"[37] which isolates the believer from other Christians and stunts growth. He goes on to explain that "the church is a community in which Christians are to live and experience much of their Christianity."[38] Whitney explains why we should go to church and why we should engage in the spiritual disciplines.

---

[36] John Alsup, "Prayer, Consciousness, and the Early Church: A Look at Acts 2:41-47 for Today," *Austin Seminary Bulletin* 4, no. 101 (1985): 31-37.

[37] Donald S. Whitney, *Spiritual Disciplines within the Church: Participating Fully in the Body of Christ.* (Chicago, IL: Moody Publishers, 1996), 13.

[38] Ibid., 14.

It's About Relationships

As we observe, significant work has already been undertaken on the subject of spiritual disciplines, delving into their definition and their profound impact on an individual's life and the communities they influence. With this knowledge, we understand that our connections with God and one another should flourish and expand considerably as we actively engage in these spiritual practices.

Forgiveness is not something we do for other people. We do it for ourselves to get well and move on. –www.lifehappy.com

Chapter Two

The Reason We Stay Broken and Disconnected

IT IS SAID that reconciling relationships "requires relating to a group of people on a human level, while at the same time [...] it involves addressing the complex needs of people whose lives reflect the social dysfunctions of our time."[39] "Dysfunction" is a word that is a frequently utilized term in the world of pastoral care. Often we identify whatever we think was not right in our lives as dysfunctional. Case in point: if a struggling mother locks the food pantry door after setting out what she deems enough for the children until she comes home from work. For some, that may be neglecting or starving the children, while to others, that may appear as a way to ensure there will be food at the end of the week. *Merriam-Webster's Collegiate Dictionary* simply defines it as "impaired, abnormal functioning, or abnormal or

---

[39] David G. Benner and Peter C. Hill, eds., *Baker Encyclopedia of Psychology & Counseling*, Baker Reference Library (Grand Rapids, MI: Baker Books, 1999), 209.

unhealthy interpersonal behavior or interaction within a group."[40] Dysfunctional or abnormal is identified by each individual person. Therefore, abnormal or unhealthy is almost, if not totally, impossible to avoid in the family life, in relationships, and in the body of believers.

Looking at reconciling relationships, we will take a bird's eye view of the family. "In Bible times, the family was comprised of members of a household including not only parents and children, along with other relatives and concubines; but also servants, travelers, aliens, and anyone else who happened to be within the house."[41] We are born into a family physically which may have been dysfunctional for various different reasons. When we leave the family nest, we take that dysfunction with us wherever we go, and ultimately, we become dysfunctional members of society and of the Church. In his book, *Care for the Chronically Wounded*, Matthew Woodley identifies the wounded as people who "represent a growing subgroup in our increasingly dysfunctional society," who are often traumatized by abuse, abandonment, or family dysfunction."[42]

---

[40] Inc Merriam-Webster, *Merriam-Webster's Collegiate Dictionary*. (Springfield, MA: Merriam-Webster, Inc., 2003). http://www.merriam-webster.com/dictionary/dysfunction (accessed Oct 12, 2013).

[41] Walter A. Elwell and Barry J. Beitzel, *Baker Encyclopedia of the Bible* (Grand Rapids, MI: Baker Book House, 1988), 767-768.

[42] Matthew Woodley, "Care for the Chronically Wounded," in *Building Your Church through Counsel and Care: 30 Strategies to Transform Your Ministry*, vol. 3, Library of Leadership Development (Minneapolis, MN: Bethany House, 1997), 244.

The Reason We Stay Broken and Disconnected

The Bible brings to light many examples of dysfunctional society. Among the more notable illustrations are found in the conflicts of Cain and Abel, Jacob and Esau, Joseph and his brothers, Saul and David, Tamar and Amnon, Mary and Martha, Paul and Barnabas, and Paul and Alexander. Identifying these conflicts as interpersonal, the *Holman Illustrated Bible Dictionary* states, "the root cause of interpersonal conflict is sin."[43] In addressing the sin with the disciplines laid out in the Bible, there is an opportunity to correct conflict and change the societal dysfunction. In *Cultivating Wholeness*, Margaret Kornfeld writes that community is where people are able to resolve conflict. She furthermore defines conflict as "to differ, to clash, to be at odds, to fight."[44] If we are placed in the community and have a model to address our sin or dysfunction and conflict, we will be able to move toward reconciled relationships.

In his book, *Connecting: Healing for Ourselves and Our Relationships a Radical New Vision*, Larry Crabb proposes that "the greatest need in modern civilization is the development of communities—true communities where the heart of God is home, where the humble and wise learn to shepherd those on the path behind them, where trusting

---

[43] *Holman Illustrated Bible Dictionary*, s.v. "Conflict, Interpersonal," Page 330.

[44] Margaret Kornfeld, *Cultivating Wholeness: A Guide to Care and Counseling in Faith Communities* (New York, NY: Bloomsbury Academic, 2000), 23.

strugglers lock arms with others are together they journey on."[45] The local body of believers should be able to provide this type of community. We are charged to find ways "internally to overcome division and enmity and to provide unity and peace, and the danger of fratricide must yield at least to concord, if not to full brotherhood."[46]

What the Bible Says

The purpose of this model is to help individuals develop biblically-based habits for reconciling relationships. It should serve as a practical guide for the daily application of spiritual disciplines to help with conflicts and lack of communication with a specific relationship. The biblical segment of this model will present an analysis of Genesis 50:15-21, which deals with the discourse between Joseph and his brothers on forgiveness, and Act 2:42-47, which deals with the development of the community of believers after Jesus' ascension.

---

[45] Larry Cabb, *Connecting: Healing for Ourselves and Our Relationships a Radical New Vision* (Nashville, TN: Word Publishing, 1997), xvii.

[46] Leon Kass, *The Beginning of Wisdom: Reading Genesis* (Chicago, IL: The University of Chicago Press, 2003), 510.

Joseph and His Brothers

The Old Testament focus will examine the relationship of the patriarchal family of Joseph, the son of Jacob, and his brothers from Genesis 50:15-21. The Book of Genesis introduces all the questions and problems that are addressed in the rest of the Bible. The roots of redemption are planted deep in Genesis, and he who would understand God's grand plan for the ages must spend much time exploring the contents of this book.[47] As a book of firsts, Genesis introduces the first man, the first woman, the first family, the first murder, and it presents the first opportunity for reverence, praise, and extends worship to the God of creation.

In order to obtain clarity from the focal pericope, we must review the basic historical narrative of Jacob and his sons, which is found in earlier chapters and throughout the Book of Genesis. The focal element of the collection is the story of Joseph, while the remaining elements gravitate to that story, adapting the plot as a framework without contributing intrinsic structural bonds to its development.[48] Charles T. Fritsch paints a picture of the later chapters of Genesis:

---

[47] James E. Smith, *The Pentateuch,* 2nd ed (Joplin, MO: College Press Publishing Company, Inc., 1993), 33.

[48] George W. Coats, "Redactional unity in Genesis 37-50," *Journal of Biblical Literature* 93 no. 1, MR (1974), 15.

> This most artistically conceived biography of the Old Testament belongs to the 'novelle' form of literary composition. The hero of the story is Joseph, whose life and character are delineated by the writer in such detail that more is known about him than any other character in the Old Testament, with the possible exception David. He is pictured as the ideal of Hebrew manhood, the model of perfect conduct in every situation. He is the favorite son of his father. He is the outstanding one of the sons, the ideal servant and prisoner, and the only one who can administer successfully Egypt's colossal food and relief program. He is unusually successful in everything he does because he fears God and his heart is pure.[49]

The genre of the story unfolds like a dramatic family narrative, which is discussed in the chapters leading to our focal passage. This project focuses on the last chapter in the Book of Genesis 50:15-21:

---

[49] Charles T. Fritsch, "God was with him: a theological study of the Joseph narrative," *Interpretation 9*, no. 1 (Jan 1955) 21.

Realizing that their father was dead, Joseph's brothers said, 'What if Joseph still bears a grudge against us and pays us back in full for all the wrong that we did to him?' So they approached Joseph, saying, 'Your father gave this instruction before he died, 'Say to Joseph: I beg you, forgive the crime of your brothers and the wrong they did in harming you.' Now therefore please forgive the crime of the servants of the God of your father.' Joseph wept when they spoke to him. Then his brothers also wept, fell down before him, and said, 'We are here as your slaves.' But Joseph said to them, 'Do not be afraid! Am I in the place of God? Even though you intended to do harm to me, God intended it for good, in order to preserve a numerous people, as he is doing today. So have no fear; I myself will provide for you and your little ones.' In this way he reassured them, speaking kindly to them.[50]

The Book of Genesis illustrates the love God shows to the people of God that no words could begin to explain the depth of its true meaning. "The reconciliation that

---

[50] Gen. 50:15-21 (New Revised Standard Version).

appeared elusive for the patriarchal generation came to some fruition through Joseph."[51] God takes the time to show us not only the beginning but also the end. Essentially, we find chapters forty-nine and fifty of Genesis sandwiched together to present a mirror of events that are two pictures of the family life that bring closure to each other. In *Genesis as a Dialogue*, Thomas L. Brodie indicates that the last two chapters are literary units or diptychs.[52] The two chapters give a touching historical account of the conclusion of the family's patriarch's life, and present the leadership of a discarded and lost brother who helped deliver the family from their bondage and possible starvation.

In this text, we find Joseph's brothers, with the goal of separating him from his family, sell him to the "highest bidder." However, as events unfold, the text reveals that his brothers could not use a few coins to sell who Joseph really was. The coins could not sell his lineage, and they could not sell his values. "Joseph's life had a greater plan as he rises to power, he reconciles his family and sustains the livelihood of people all over the world."[53] As we approach this chapter, Jacob, Joseph's father has died. When Joseph's brethren realized the heinousness of their crime, they readily confessed

---

[51] George W. Coats, "Joseph, Son of Jacob," in *The Anchor Bible, Vol 1*, ed. David Noel Freedman (New York, NY: Doubleday, 1992), 978.

[52] Brodie Thomas, *Genesis a Dialogue: A Literary, Historical, and Theological Commentary*
(New York, NY: Oxford Press, 2001), xxvi.

[53] Coates, 981.

and begged his forgiveness.[54] It is compelling to observe the need for the brothers to gain the forgiveness of Joseph. As cited by Sinclair:

> Seventeen years has past. The family has settled in Egypt, where they are richly blessed. As God intended in Genesis, they are fruitful and they 'multiply exceedingly.' Joseph's sons, Ephraim and Manasseh, are adopted by Jacob. Finally, after a long and eventful life, Jacob blesses his children on his deathbed. With Jacob's death comes a major shift in the family dynamic.[55]

It almost appears as if they have now digressed since Joseph had already welcomed them into what was now his home. Nevertheless, among themselves, they discussed the possible grudge Joseph may have against them.

A word used in the pericope is "grudge" (*satam*), which means to bear a grudge or cherish animosity against.[56] "Frequently found in the earliest translations *satam*, this word was altered in newer versions to 'murmur' ***nāṭar***

---

[54] Ibid, 29.

[55] Celia Sinclair, *Genesis* (Louisville, KY: Westminster Press, 1999), 88.

[56] R. L. Thomas, *New American Standard Hebrew-Aramaic and Greek Dictionaries* (Anaheim: Foundations Publications, Inc., 1998), Logos Bible Software.

which means to keep anger."[57] The same word is used when describing how Esau held a grudge against his brother Jacob for stealing his birthright. The end of this saga reverts to feelings of guilt and it reveals the brother's conscience.[58] It appears as if the brothers were unable to rid themselves of the sense of guilt incurred when Joseph was still a boy. When the brothers appealed to Joseph, maybe they began to reflect on the way they treated him so many years ago. The word can also be translated as persecute or hate.[59] If Joseph wanted to retaliate or punish them for their actions, their fate would have been doomed, so they thought. Maybe Joseph had a hidden hatred that had not surfaced when their father was alive, but now he may show his true feelings.[60] We might also notice that prior to this request, nowhere in the text do the brothers ask for forgiveness and it seems to be inconceivable to them that Joseph would not require any penance on their part.[61] Unable or afraid to face their brother, they send him a note [vv. 16-17] inferring instructions from their father Jacob. In this note is a request for forgiveness

---

[57] J. D. Douglas, "Grudge," ed. D. R. W. Wood et al., *New Bible Dictionary* (Leicester, England; Downers Grove, IL: InterVarsity Press, 1996), 436.

[58] Gerhard Von Rad, 431.

[59] J. Strong, *Concise Dictionary of the Words in the Greek Testament and the Hebrew Bible*, vol. 2a (Bellingham, WA: Logos Bible Software, 2009), 115.

[60] K. A. Mathews, *The New American Commentary, Genesis 11:27-50:26*, vol. 1b (Nashville, TN: Broadman & Holman Publishers, 2005), 904.

[61] Ibid., 925.

and an admission of guilt which are key ingredients in the process of reconciliation.

The word "forgive," according to *Strong's Exhaustive Concordance of the Bible,* is the Hebrew word *nasa*, which means (v.17) "to bear, to lift up, forgive." Typically, God is always the subject of forgiveness (*salah*).[62] Forgiveness is defined as "the wiping out of an offense from memory." As noted by *The Anchor Bible Dictionary*, once the offense is eradicated, there should not be any problem between the offenders and the offended, and they should live in restored harmony. The request was to wipe the slate clean as if the offense had never happened.[63] To forgive is to exercise love, and love is action. Soren Kierkegaard indicated that "love hides a multiplicity of sins by forgiveness." Forgiveness as love points to God's compassion, which ignites the forgiving process beyond human understanding.[64] We are able to see forgiveness actually occurs when the offended removes the burden and offense, which generally warrants punishment.[65]

---

[62] W. E. Vine, Merrill F. Unger, and William White Jr., "To Forgive" in *Vine's Complete Expository Dictionary of Old and New Testament Words* (Nashville: Thomas Nelson Publisher, 1984), 86.

[63] John S. Kselman, "Forgiveness" in *The Anchor Bible Dictionary*, vol. 2, ed. David Noel Freedman (New York, NY: Doubleday, 1992), 831.

[64] Carnegie Samuel Calian. 1981. "Christian faith as forgiveness." *Theology Today* 37, no. 4: 439-443. *ATLA Religion Database with ATLASerials*, EBSCO*host* (accessed February 6, 2014).

[65] Stephen Westerholm, "Forgiveness," in *The New Interpreter's Dictionary of the Bible,* vol. 2, ed. Katherine Doob Sakenfeld (Nashville, TN: Abingdon Press, 2007), 481.

The brothers finally acknowledged their sins and asked for forgiveness for their misdeeds. In response, Joseph wept (v.17b). His cry could indicate that his understanding of God was so vastly different from his brothers. Baldwin provides a dialogue on how Joseph was shaped and developed through God's particular dealings with him by "enabling him to endure hardship, resist temptation and keep hopeful even when other people let him down."[66] The hand of God in the life of Joseph allowed him to see the plan beyond the pain. "It was clear that he found the motivation and the power to forgive through God's dealings with him."[67] This time of crying may have marked a move toward resolving the conflict by indicating that Joseph had no intention of seeking revenge.[68] However, Calian reports that forgiveness of sin has proven to be a costly affair. When we look to the cross, we acknowledge reconciliation is impossible without suffering and impossible without God. However, as "we receive and remember God's costly mercies, we are motivated to practice costly reconciliation with others."[69]

The tearful scene moves to the brothers coming before Joseph and falling down before him (v.18). The interesting

---

[66] Joyce Baldwin, *The Message of Genesis 12-50: From Abraham to Joseph* (Downers Grove, IL: Varsity Press, 1986), 218.

[67] Ibid., 219.

[68] Fretheim, 671.

[69] Carnegie, 439-443.

thing Joseph does is address their fears of his retaliation. "Don't be afraid," he says, not once, but twice (v. 19, 21). The plan of God to reconcile and deliver is sandwiched in these verses. Paul Hanson speaks to the social and anthropological methods identifying how individuals in Genesis draw on oral ancestral traditions learned about Yahweh God.[70] Social anthropology is "described as a distinctive style of anthropology—comparative, fieldwork-based, with strong intellectual links to the sociological ideas of Émile Durkheim."[71] Social anthropology is often contrasted with "cultural anthropology, a major division of anthropology that deals with the study of culture in all of its aspects and that uses the methods, concepts, and data of archaeology, ethnography, ethnology, folklore, and linguistics in its descriptions and analyses of the diverse peoples of the world."[72] From the social anthropology lens, it could be determined that Joseph draws on the oral traditions of God by using God's love and compassion to address his siblings. The entire ordeal shows how Joseph takes the focus off men and puts it on God. Gerhard Von Rad indicates that

---

[70] Paul D. Hanson, *The People Called: The Growth of Community in the Bible* (San Francisco, CA: Harper & Row Publisher, 1986), 15.

[71] "Social Anthropology," in *Encyclopedia Britannica* from Encyclopedia Britannica Online. http://www.britannica.com/EBchecked/topic/1072704/social-anthropology (accessed November 2, 2013).

[72] "Cultural Anthropology", in *Encyclopedia Britannica* from Encyclopedia Britannica Online. http://www.britannica.com/EBchecked/topic/146165/cultural-anthropology (accessed November 2, 2013).

there are two important things revealed: "one he defines his relationship to God, and the other that of his brother's relationship to God."[73] The text, "Am I in the place of God?" indicates that God is the controller of our fate. "In Joseph's explanation, God's forgiveness, which leads to reconciliation, is joined to actions which save the lives of many."[74] The thought of retaliation does not appear to be the intent because he understands God's purpose. Joseph goes on to say his brother meant evil, but God meant good (v. 20). Joseph's actions and comments display a great comprehension of God's promises to Abraham, Isaac and Jacob. It is that "Because God is sovereign and faithful" and has accomplished the preservation of his people in the past, Joseph is sure of God's plan for his future.[75] "The God who created the world and called it good has been about life and its preservation in and through all of these events, despite their intentions for

death."[76] Joseph advises his brothers that God allowed the many turns of events in his life for "the saving of many lives." Blenkinsopp states, "Here we have from the prophetic Elohist source, the profoundly original idea that

---

[73] Gerhard Von Rad, 432.

[74] Claus Westermann, *Genesis 37-50: A Continental Commentary* (Minneapolis, MN: Fortress Press, 2002), 205.

[75] Sidney Greidanus, *Preaching Christ From Genesis* (Grand Rapids, MI: William B. Eerdmans Publishing, 2007), 460.

[76] Fretheim, 672.

even the consequences of bad will and moral weakness can be caught up and transformed in the divine plan."[77]

The last statement shared with the brothers is one of reassurance of their provision. The brothers have acknowledged their sin. Joseph leads them to divine knowledge about the Creator God being the director of all human affairs. The family is now reconciled. Joseph says, "I will provide for you and your children," thus further assuring his brothers there is no malice, only a desire to be reconciled with his family. Matthews reports that Joseph concludes his speech by promising to perpetuate the necessities of life that he had afforded since Jacob's arrival in Egypt, noting especially that he himself will see to this.[78] Joseph's statement proposes an example of responsibility and benevolence toward his brothers. God's redemptive purpose for Israel and the world was carried forward in the life and character of Joseph.[79] God's plan triumphs all of our desires and detours while continuously reconciling. Walter Brueggemann provides this observation:

> The listening community may here reflect on the inscrutable way in which the purposes of God supersede the best human

---

[77] Joseph Blenkinsopp and John Challenor, *Scripture Discussion Commentary: Pentateuch* (Chicago, IL: ACTA Foundation, 1971), 131.

[78] Mathews, 927-928.

[79] Fritsch, 33.

> plans. On the one hand, that is an assurance that we may trust ourselves to God's transcendent purposes. On the other hand, it warns us that our plans are provisional and 'subject to review.' The deepest of human intentions are set in the context of God's unyielding intent.[80]

As we conclude and reflect on the Old Testament pericope and reconciling relationships, it is determined that "Genesis serves as an introduction to the Mosaic Law and it begins the history of redemption that occupies the rest of the Bible."[81] In the Old Testament, two word groups convey the idea of redemption. The verb *ga'al* and its cognates mean "to buy back" or "to redeem."[82] Through Joseph's display of faith and understanding of God's commands and spiritual disciplines as given through the ancestral stories that give him the fortitude to persevere through wrongdoings perpetrated against him. In his book, *Joseph's Memoirs*, Hugh Rowe gives the reader a perspective from the eyes of Joseph as he walks through the life of this great Patriarch.

---

[80] Walter Brueggemann, *Genesis: Interpretation, a Bible Commentary For Teaching and Preaching* (Atlanta, GA: Knox Press, 1982), 374.

[81] Raymond B. Dillard and Tremper Longman III, *An Introduction to the Old Testament* (Grand Rapids, MI: Zondervan, 1994), 51.

[82] Stan Norman, "Redeem, Redemption, Redeemer," ed. Chad Brand et al., *Holman Illustrated Bible Dictionary* (Nashville, TN: Holman Bible Publishers, 2003), 1370.

Rowe has the young Joseph reflect on his life where he points straight to the family Patriarch, Abraham. "It all began with my great grandfather Abram and the lesson he taught his son Isaac, who saw the value in these lessons and continued teaching them to his son, my father, who then passed them on to his children."[83] Joseph, through ordered steps, landed in Egypt, a different culture and environment, and perhaps a place where God appeared absent. Yet he refused to allow the circumstances to change who he was internally. This pericope "gives us an opportunity to examine the character of Joseph, now that he is away from the sheltering presence of his doting father."[84] Through his many trials, he remained true to his faith and the belief system God taught him by his ancestors. "Faith is the beginning of everything. It is the fuel that keeps us going and believing."[85]

In the opinion of the writer, we come to the understanding that God had reconciliation in mind from the beginning. In his book, *The Post Black & Post White Church*, Efrem Smith points to the Garden of Eden, where in the beginning, God said that man should not be alone, that His plan is to make a covenant with Abraham who will lead

---

[83] Hugh Rowe, *Joseph's Memoirs: Life Lesson for a Successful You* (Bloomington, IN: Author House, 2012), 1.

[84] Leon Kass, *The Beginning of Wisdom* (Chicago, IL: The University Press, 2003), 539.

[85] Rowe, 13.

a community of individuals called the children of Israel.[86] Beverly Flanigan interjects the following thought pattern:

> In primitive societies and in centuries past people had to rely on each other. Members of tribes or clans depended on one another to meet their most basic need. Procurement of food, clothing, shelter, and safety was impossible without the cooperative efforts of each member. Each individual played a role essential to the survival of the whole. The loss of one person threatened the survival of all.[87]

Reflecting on Joseph's reconciliation should provide valuable lessons: "to refuse to forgive is to distance ourselves from God and to cut ourselves off from that possibility"[88] of being in relationship with God and with others. Joseph does not allow his circumstances to make him bitter. Therefore, in forgiving, he thought of reconciliation as God's plan. This conviction led him to say to his

---

[86] Efrem Smith, *The Post Black & Post White Church* (San Francisco, CA: Jossey-Bass, 2012), 30.

[87] Beverly Flanigan, *Forgiving the Unforgivable* (New York, NY: Collier Books, 1992), 7.

[88] Lance Stone, "Forgiveness," *Journal for Preachers*, 29, no. 2 (2006): 46. *ATLA Religion Database with ATLASerials*, EBSCO*host* (accessed March 21, 2012).

brothers, "you intended to harm me, but God intended it for good to accomplish what is not being done, the saving of many lives."[89]

Forgiveness is not only for oneself or one's accuser but also for the entire community. This is what helps you to understand why forgiveness and reconciliation are used in the same sentence. In *Forgiving and Reconciling*, Everett Worthington presents this very thought process:

> Theologian David Augsbeger has argued for years that forgiveness is intended to include reconciliation. He suggests that in biblical times the Hebrews did not parse forgiveness into mere emotional forgiveness. Rather, biblical forgiveness was meant to include both the intrapersonal and the interpersonal. He treats forgiveness as an inclusive term that I would say involves both forgiveness and reconciliation. What I call emotional forgiveness he calls agape love: what I call reconciliation, he calls forgiveness.[90]

---

[89] Gen. 50:20 (Revised Standard Version).

[90] Everett L. Worthington Jr., *Forgiving and Reconciling: Bridges to Wholeness and Hope* (Downers Grove, IL: Inter Varsity Press, 2003), 68.

Joseph uses his life circumstances to make himself stronger, to work harder, and to address his intrapersonal and interpersonal self. He does this through serving others better, sharing his knowledge willingly, and striving to be prepared to provide for those in need, which he believed was God's plan and purpose for his life. "Once the brothers come to recognize and acknowledge this, forgiveness and reconciliation can follow. Many people are kept alive (rescued from death.)"[91] This divine plan was not an afterthought. It was the design from the beginning of time. As Von Rad sums up, "Even when no man could imagine it God has all the strings in his hand."[92] In his book, *From Healing to Hurt,* Andrew Park identifies what is believed to be meant by "God has all the strings in his hand." Park proposes two very specific themes that consume his last chapter: "God is deeply present" and "God has a plan."[93] This is good news. When we are in the midst of a struggle and cannot see the end, we must remember God is with us and God knows the outcome.

---

[91] Blenkinsopp, 133.

[92] Hillel L. Millgram, *The Joseph Paradox: A Radical Reading of Genesis 37-50* (Jefferson, NC: McFarland & Company, Inc., 2012), 199.

[93] Andrew Sung Park, *From Hurt to Healing: a Theology of the Wounded* (Nashville, TN:
Abingdon Press, 2004), 141.

The New Community

The beliefs, life, and sacrifices of the early followers of Christ give us endless testimonies of pioneers who were reconciled to God, who formed relationships, who developed spiritually, and who practiced discipline. The word "reconciled," according to the *Encyclopedic Dictionary of the Bible*, is a synonym of the word "atonement," which means "literally the setting at one of two or more persons who were at odds with each other" as long as you keep in mind "reconciliation is generally between one who has been offended and one who has given the offense."[94]

In an attempt to provide a greater understanding of this subject matter, the Acts of the Apostles will be utilized to demonstrate how the early church formed and prospered in the Lord. Specifically, in the focal text of Acts 2:42-47:

> They devoted themselves to the apostles' teaching and fellowship, to the breaking of bread and the prayers. Awe came upon everyone, because many wonders and signs were being done by the apostles. All who believed were together and had all things in common; they would sell their possessions and goods and distribute the

---

[94] *Encyclopedic Dictionary of the Bible* (New York, NY: McGraw-Hill Book Company, 1963), s.v. "Reconciled," 167.

> proceeds to all, as any had need. Day by day, as they spent much time together in the temple, they broke bread at home and ate their food with glad and generous hearts, praising God and having the goodwill of all the people. And day by day the Lord added to their number those who were being saved.[95]

The Acts of the Apostles is the book directly following the four gospels in the New Testament and appears to be a continuation of the story written between

A.D. 62 and 64, according to Guthrie.[96] This book is the unfolding of the work of Jesus Christ as those who converted to Christianity form a community of people called the Church. "The church of Acts is a community of goods. It is a united witness to the Messiah's resurrection, which is not only proclaimed but is also embodied in its common life under the aegis of the Holy Spirit."[97] Identified as The Acts of the Apostles, it provides a picture of the beginnings of the Church. The Book of Acts gives the Christians of

---

[95] Acts 2:42-47 (Revised Standard Version).

[96] David Fiensy, *The College Press NIV Commentary New Testament* Introduction (Joplin, MO: College Press Publishing, 1994) 161.

[97] *The New Interpreter's Bible: A Commentary in Twelve Volumes*, vol. 10, ed. Leander E. Keck, William Lane, and Marion Soards (Nashville, TN: Abingdon Press, 2002), 23.

The Reason We Stay Broken and Disconnected

today basic information and insight to the early church.[98] It is a book of examples to be followed by every believer, every church body, and the universal church. Early church tradition indicates Acts and the third Gospel were written by Luke, a traveling companion and fellow worker of the apostle Paul. Elwell and Comfort refer to Luke as "the beloved physician" and mentioned among Paul's coworkers.[99] Gonzalez states that the purpose of this book is to show how the Holy Spirit allows the Church to discover and rediscover its mission.[100] In the book of Acts, Jesus leaves them with the words "you will be my witnesses" all over the world.

In our focal passage, we find a group of individuals identified as believers who have received the power of the Holy Spirit. This new distinction is assigned to all of those who were disciples of Jesus and/or heard the message of the gospel from Peter. They converted from Judaism to Christianity and turned their lives over to the way of Jesus Christ. This is a devotion to the one true and living God. Through the bold evangelistic efforts of Peter, many came to Christ and now the passage has presented a view of common living amongst the new disciples.

---

[98] Walvoord, 349.

[99] W. A. Elwell and P. W. Comfort, *Tyndale Bible Dictionary* (Wheaton, IL: Tyndale House Publishers, 2001), 11.

[100] Justo L. Gonzalez, *Acts: The Gospel of the Spirit* (Maryknoll, NY: Orbis Books, 2001), 49.

This periscope describes the earliest days of the Church at Jerusalem and the new Messianic movement.[101] Luke takes the opportunity to give a description of the early church (v. 42) by listing their distinguishing markers, namely, devotion to the apostles teaching, fellowship with one another, breaking of bread, and prayer. In a sense "repentance and baptism have made a community" of saints ready to dedicate themselves to their Savior and Lord.[102] G. Campbell Morgan identifies the four disciplines, that is, devotion to the apostles' teaching, fellowship, breaking bread, and prayer, as ordinances. He makes it clear that repentance and baptism are not ordinances of Christian fellowship but are ordinances of entrance into the fellowship.[103] Those who believed in Peter's message are being identified by their participation in what can be summed up as the spiritual disciplines. Dallas Willard claims that we need to develop what is an ongoing spiritual presence with the Kingdom of God that at the same time connects us to our psychological reality.[104]

---

[101] Richard N. Longenecker, *The Expositor's Bible Commentary: John and Acts* (Grand Rapids, MI: Zondervan, 1981), 288-289.

[102] Robert Maddox, *The Laymen's Bible Book Commentary: Acts* (Nashville, TN: Broadman Press, 1979), 32.

[103] G. Campbell Morgan, *The Acts of the Apostles* (Old Tappan, NJ: Fleming H. Revell Company, 1924), 92.

[104] Dallas Willard, *The Spirit of the Disciplines: Understanding How God Changes Lives* (New York: Harper Collins Publishers, 1988), xi.

In the text, the disciplines are teaching and fellowshipping (sharing with one another), breaking bread ("participation of one loaf and cup communion"[105] or a "technical term for the Eucharist"[106]), and praying (the daily practice of this new community.) "Each is a concrete expression of forgiveness of sins and the reception of the Spirit—made possible only because of conversion—and the practices are too demanding for an individual. Therefore, initial images of conversion in Acts are those of a community and of shared practices and goods."[107] As we reflect on reconciliation, we must understand the various disciplines. In these disciplines, we find perseverance, repetition, corporation, partners, fellowship, and "solidarity and the sharing of feelings, goods, and actions."[108]

The new community of believers could be described as a reflection of our biological families due to their daily proximity to each other. In addition, Acts 2 is proven evidence by George Woodbey that the "social practices of the early community lay a basis for supporting socialist ideals of cooperative living because all things in common

---

[105] G. W. H. Lampe, "Communion" *The Interpreter's Dictionary of the Bible* (New York, NY: Abingdon Press, 1962), 665.

[106] Louis F. Hartman, ed. and trans. *Encyclopedic Dictionary of the Bible* (New York, NY: McGraw-Hill Book Company, 1963), 665.

[107] *The New Interpreter's Bible*, vol. 10, 73.

[108] Justo L. Gonzalez, *Acts: The Gospel of the Spirit* (Maryknoll, NY: Orbis Books, 2001), 51.

provided economic equality."[109] However, the community formed not only to satisfy the need for material but also to get to know God through their fellowship with the Word and believers. "The fellowship in spiritual things had its outcome in other fellowship: the fellowship of goods, fellowship in worship—they continued in the temple worshipping; fellowship in the home life—from house to house they passed in social inter-relationship."[110] For the most part, these people had lived in the same towns together all their lives, but now they would have more in common. They would now grow to have one God and one faith in common. The way to develop this new commonality starts in the Book of Acts. The believers are to yield or devote their lives to the apostles' teaching, fellowship with one another, breaking of bread, and prayer.

The word that introduces these disciplines is "devoted." Luke uses the word "devoted" (*proskartereo*), which means steadfast and single-minded toward a certain course of action.[111] The believers now directed by the spirit devote themselves to this new way of living. While evangelism was certainly an aspect of the Christian life, the primary purpose of their common life is to nurture Christian community.[112] This persistence and continuance in the apostle's presence was most

---

[109] Brian Blount, *True to Our Native Land: An African American New Testament* (Minneapolis: Fortress Press, 2007), 221-22.

[110] G. Campbell Morgan, 93.

[111] Longenecker, 289.

[112] Wall, 71.

likely necessary for their spiritual growth. The focus of their time, resources, and attention should be on specific behavior patterns that will lead to unity of the body of believers and a lifetime relationship with God. Saint Cyprian of Carthage believed Luke was referencing the

> 'common mind [that] prevailed once, in the time of the Apostles,' as this 'common mind' was documented in the opening chapters of Acts, 'God is one, and Christ is one, and His Church is one; one is the faith, and one the people cemented together by harmony into the strong unity of a body.[113]

The concept was also captured by the apostle Paul throughout his writings as indicated by Michael Gorman in *Apostle of the Crucified Lord*. Gorman follows Paul's writings on the Church being a holy community "constantly depicted as a fellowship—a community with common concerns and a common mission—and a family of brothers and sisters."[114] The community stands out in the environment in which it lives "distant from the host culture and within the church there is to be an ethos of harmony, humility, and above all

---

[113] Jaroslav Pelikan, *Brazos Theological Commentary of the Bible: Acts* (Grand Rapids, IL: Brazo Press, 2005), 58.

[114] Michael J. Gorman, *Apostle of the Crucified Lord: A Theological Introduction to Paul & His Letters* (Grand Rapids, MI: William B. Eerdmans Publishing Company, 2004), 127.

love—not only towards siblings in the faith but toward outsiders and enemies as well."[115]

The first discipline is the studying of the apostles' teaching: "chiefly it was, supposed to be their personal recollections of Jesus and his teachings."[116] They were steadfast in the practice of the renewing of their minds in the Word of God. This teaching was authoritative because it was the teaching of the Lord communicated through the apostles in the power of the Holy Spirit.[117] The early church members were the true picture of a disciple. They studied the Word and practiced the Word. Their discipleship was identified as a group effort, therefore it was imperative that believers come together to study the Word of God. We should also note the teaching of the apostles linked to the signs and wonders they performed in the same chapter.[118] Their continued study helped them accomplish the directive to "go and make disciples."

The second discipline identified is fellowship, a term more commonly known in the Greek language as *koinonia*, the gathering of people in community. In this community, one was made strong through the presence of others and the encouragement of one another. Translations of the

---

[115] Gorman, 141.

[116] *The Interpreter's Bible, Vol. IX, ed.* George Arthur Buttrick et. al (New York, NY: Abingdon Press, 1954), 50.

[117] F. F. Bruce, *The Book of Acts* (Grand Rapids, MI: William B. Eerdmans Publishing Company, 1988), 73.

[118] Mikeal C. Parsons, *Acts (Paideia: Commentaries on the New Testament)*, (Grand Rapids: Baker Publishing Group, 2008), 48.

term *koinonia* include "communion, fellowship, and sharing in common."[119] From this term, we gather the true sense of sharing everything they had with one another. Explaining this term economically, we see "the community reorders its possessions [...] so that its generosity toward the needy reciprocates God's generosity in the gift of salvation."[120]

However, this passage stretches beyond a meal and breaking bread, which is the next discipline. This passage speaks to the devotion of the people to ensure everyone has what they need to survive. The fellowship was not only in prayers or doctrine alone but also in social relations.[121] It goes beyond just the people we like and includes the entire body of believers. Malina states:

> Fellowship may mean spending time together as in a social club. However, given the fact that group members did pool their resources, the word would mean that Luke is referring to the mutual obligations of partnership or association between one person and one or more other people with regard to a particular action, thing or person. It is a type of informal partnership contract. Partners were

---

[119] Vine, 233.

[120] *The New Interpreter's Bible*, 23.

[121] Jaroslav Pelikan, *Acts: Brazos Theological Commentary on the Bible* (Grand Rapids: Baker Publishing Group, 2005), 59.

> obligated to support the project of the group
> from their resources.[122]

This passage focuses on a command and the actual unfolding of the disciplines. The believer learned the discipline through the word, and then engaged in doing them through deeds and application on a daily basis.

The word "communion" is also identified as *koinonia*, translated as "sharing," and is used in the New Testament for the sharing of believers in fellowship together and with God.[123] They had the opportunity to share what resources they had with a sense of unity, and to spend time in praise and worship of the Lord. Although there is a community, there is a clear distinction between corporate worship and a time of private worship in the home-fellowship (vv. 42, 46).

They devoted themselves to the breaking of bread. This discipline was one they embarked upon during the time of fellowship. The omission of "and" between "fellowship" and "to breaking of bread and to prayer" indicates the last two activities are appositional to fellowship.[124] Therefore, when they came together for fellowship, they engaged in the sharing of resources and broke bread. As indicated previously, Luke mentions breaking of bread twice "here possibly a distinction

---

[122] Bruce J. Malina, *Social Science Commentary on the Book of Acts* (Minneapolis, MN: Fortress Press, 2008), 36.

[123] Dennis E. Smith, "Communion," *in The New Interpreter's Dictionary of the Bible*, vol. 1 (Nashville, TN: Abington, 1976), 711.

[124] Walvoord, 360.

between a regular meal (partook of food) and Eucharistic rite (breaking of bread) is suggested, even though originally both were integrated into one event."[125] This is another form of worship, the breaking of bread. This is Lukan shorthand for the Lord's Supper and refers to one aspect of the corporate worship of the early church.[126] Therefore, breaking of bread, eating together, and sharing in the Lord's Supper has been for centuries, and should be now at the center of the Christian church.

According to the passage, Christians persevered both in their attendance at the Temple (the new worship as Jews, which they all were) and in breaking bread, (the new form of Christian worship that was developing).[127] These were times of concern because the Church was experiencing persecution. However, "dining together created a tie or bond among the diners which in turn created an ethical obligation toward them."[128] In the face of the trials, knowing they had a risen Savior should have warmed their hearts to carry on with the mission, making this time of breaking bread one of joy and anticipation for the future in the Savior's presence.

---

[125] "The Breaking of Bread," in *The Anchor Bible Dictionary*, vol. 4, ed. David Noel Freedman (New York, NY: Doubleday, 1992), 366.

[126] Mikeal C. Parsons, *Acts* (Grand Rapids, IL: Baker Publishing Group, 2008), 49.

[127] Gonzalez, 51.

[128] Smith, "Dining Together," in *The Anchor Bible Dictionary*, vol. 2, ed. David Noel Freedman (New York, NY: Doubleday, 1992) 302.

It's About Relationships

As with the breaking of bread, prayer is identified as an essential discipline for the early church. A classic definition of Christian prayer is an offering up of our desires unto God, for things agreeable to his will, in the name of Christ, with confession of our sins, and thankful acknowledgement of his mercies (Westminster Shorter Catechism).[129] Prayer was a necessary tool in the Christian community. Longenecker notes: "Just as Luke has set up in Luke–Acts the parallelism between the Spirit's work in relation to Jesus and the Spirit's work in the church, so he also sets up the parallelism between prayer in the life of Jesus and prayer in the life of the Church."[130]

If it was a practice of Jesus, surely it should be the pivot point in the life of every believer to pray day and night without ceasing. The word *proseuche* is a technical term, a request for help made to speaking to a deity, usually in the form of petition, vow, or wish prayer, but it is also used to designate the place of prayer.[131] The act of confessing our sins and the praying for one another is cleansing and it helps the believer rely on God to get them through the events of each day. However, this ordinance or discipline of prayer was systematic, definite, and positive for individuals but done in connection with one another.[132]

---

[129] W. A. Elwell and B. J. Beitzel, in *Baker encyclopedia of the Bible* (Grand Rapids, MI: Baker Book House, 1988), 1745.

[130] Longenecker, 290.

[131] *The New Interpreter's Dictionary of the Bible*, vol. 4 (Nashville, TN: Abington, 1976), s.v. "prayer," 586.

[132] Morgan, 93.

It is important to note that prayer is identified as prayer (2:42) or praise (2:47), and in describing such prayer in terms of praise, we are being told that the Church attributed all that it was and all that it had to God.[133] The connection between prayer and praise is important to understand as there is more to prayer than supplication and our petitions. Parsons explains prayer has a vertical dimension in the community praising God, and a horizontal dimension in prayer directed outward to all the people.[134] Therefore, the prayers of the believers should include prayers of thanksgiving and prayers of intercession.

As we take the opportunity to look at this community, we find that "this move to community, to people, and even to enduring institutions that carry and express our shared memories and hopes, is a central but neglected theme of the Christian faith."[135] For this reason, there is a need to bring to light the need for understanding what God meant for the Church, which is to model to the onlooker what it means to be a family. In "Acts 2:41-47 the reader finds the new community, demonstrating a commonality that is worked out in the selling of property and possessions for the benefit of everyone who had a

---

[133] Gonzalez, 54.

[134] Parsons, 49.

[135] Anthony B. Robinson & Robert Wall, *Called to Be Church* (Grand Rapids, MI: William B. Eerdmans Publishing, 2006), 4.

need."[136] They are to model what it means to be in community together, and it is evident they cannot do this through their own means. In *The Acts of the Apostles a Socio-Rhetorical Commentary*, Ben Witherington unpacks the term spiritual discipline.

> From the beginning the church linked the desire for more of God to intentional practices, relationships and experiences that gave people space in their lives to keep company with Jesus. These intentional practices, relationships and experiences were known as spiritual disciplines; which are the basic rhythm of disciplines (or rule) for the first believers are found in Acts 2:42.[137]

The spiritual disciplines laid out in the second chapter of Acts coupled with the gift and power of the Holy Spirit give us a springboard for how believers can be empowered to reconcile relationships. In conclusion, the Acts passage provides a rich foundation to facilitate a model for

---

[136] Michael A. Salmeier, *Restoring the Kingdom: The Role of God as the Ordainer of the Time and Seasons in the Acts of the Acts of the Apostles* (Eugene, OR: 2001), 124.

[137] Ben Witherington III, *The Acts of the Apostles: a Socio-Rhetorical Commentary* (Grand Rapids, MI: Wm. B. Eerdmans Publishing Company, 1998), 163.

reconciling relationships by suggesting economic change along with spiritual change. Walter Wink elaborates on this very proposal.

> Jesus' solution was neither utopian nor apocalyptic. It was simple realism. Nothing less could halt or reverse the economic decline of Jewish peasant than a complete suspension of usury and debt and a restoration of economic equality through outright grants, a pattern actually implemented in the earliest Christian community, according to the Book of Acts.[138]

The environment or community presents the perfect dynamic for fostering change and mending fences between individuals from unlimited types of cultural, ethnic, and social backgrounds. "The birth of the church was not on the basis of new theological propositions, but solely on sociological grounds—social and racial equality."[139] Through the spiritual disciplines outlined above, the new community of believers was able to understand the God in whom it now had formed allegiance. This new

---

[138] Walter Wink, *Engaging the Powers: Discernment and Resistance in a World of Domination* (Minneapolis, MN: Fortress Press, 1992), 184.

[139] Brian K. Blount, Cain Hope Felder, Clarice J. Martin, and Emerson B. Powery, eds. *True to Our Native Land: An African American New Testament Commentary* (Minneapolis, MN: Fortress Press, 2007), 215.

way of life supports not only "spiritual activities such as prayer, but also physical food or other goods in common"[140] to provide for the needs of everyone. This suggested fellowship brought about unity, which refers to a group of individuals in harmony with each other.[141] In other words, fellowship and commonality allow for an equal footing, and equality leads to an atmosphere ripe for reconciliation. Walter Wink addresses this same concern, suggesting a need for equality among the community. The community set forth in our focal text ends economic exploitation because economic inequalities can be a breeding ground for domination.[142] As we bring about a sense of equality through meeting the needs of all that come to the table, we are better equipped to help them resolve their spiritual depravity and separation from God and one another.

It Went Down In History

The whole concept of spiritual formation or application of spiritual disciplines can be seen throughout history, examined, and explained in the formation of the early church by the apostle Paul, Saint Augustine, Pope Gregory the Great, and many more. In defining practical theology, Friedrich Schleiermacher indicates that we

---

[140] Witherington III, 160.

[141] Ibid., 161.

[142] Wink, 113.

must know Christian traditions historically, exegetically, and dogmatically.[143] Restoring families and relationships through applying the spiritual disciplines found in the Word of God has been a process since the forming of the Church in Jerusalem. This is important to the Church because, as explained by Monica Hellwig, "reconciliation is the task of the whole community that is Church."[144]

Throughout history, regardless of the location, the Church has been the place where reconciliation is learned through various practices:

> Once inside, the new Christian was certainly not expected to be entirely sinless, but it was understood that the life of the community of believers would continually meditate forgiveness and conversion from 'daily sins' for its member by the Eucharistic celebration, by prayer together but also by the life and deeds of charity in the community.[145]

---

[143] James Woodward and Stephen Pattison, *The Blackwell Reader in Pastoral and Practical Theology* (Malden, MA: Blackwell Publishing, 2000), 24.

[144] Monica K. Hellwig, *Sign of Reconciliation and Conversion: The Sign of Penance for Our Time* (Wilmington, DE: Michael Glazier, Inc., 1984), 28.

[145] Ibid., 30.

Solutions to the Problem

This historical foundation will attempt to identify how historical figures and people groups have engaged in specific spiritual disciplines, such as the study of God's Word, the practice of prayer, worship, and fellowship to aid in the restoration of relationships. Spiritual disciplines as identified in this paper can be viewed as single entities as well as being lived out synonymously together. History unfolds the implementation of the various spiritual disciplines. Below we will discuss the intriguing conversations from the theologians through the periods of church history.

During the age of the apostles, church growth was rapid and application of the spiritual disciplines was daily practice. In his book, *The Church,* Mark Dever writes that worship includes God's Word, singing God's praises, and prayer. He goes on referring to the Book of Acts indicating the early Christians "devoted themselves to the apostle's teaching and to the fellowship, to the breaking of bread and to prayer."[146] This is directly from the focal passage describing the formation of the Church in Acts. Over and over, there is a clear indication of daily worship. The non-Christian Roman official Pliny, writing to Emperor Trajan, referred to the fact that Christians met regularly before daybreak on the appointed day.[147]

---

[146] Mark Dever, *The Church: The Gospel Made Visible* (Nashville, TN: B&H Academic, 2012), 71.

[147] Ibid., 136.

As we view the history of the early church from this point on, we will list some of the many contributors in acts and dialogue to the development of reconciliation and spiritual disciplines. The *First Apology* of Justin Martyr and the *Didache* indicate the continuance of the Church model. During the services, the Church would read the "memoirs of the apostles" or the "writings of the prophets," which would include a small sermon homily. They would also spend time in prayer and share in the celebration of the Lord's Supper.[148] The *Didache* is an early second-century document. Justin Martyr was writing in the middle of the second century and Hippolytus was writing in the early third century. Both referred to the fact that Christians met regularly before daybreak in local assemblies to hear God's Word read and preached, to witness faith professed in baptism, to take the Lord's Supper, to pray and to sing together, to teach and give, to encourage one another, to bear one another's burdens and sorrows, and to know and be known.[149]

Justin Maytr's *First Apology* indicates that the believers spent time offering prayers in common for themselves and for others. They presented the Eucharistic bread, wine, and water, while the deacons carried communion to whoever was absent from the assembly. Also, the prosperous, with the desire to do so, assisted those persons who were in need. They visited one another continually, reading the writings of

---

[148] Earle E. Cairns, *Christianity Through the Centuries: A History of the Christian Church* (Grand Rapids, MI: Zondervan Publishing House, 1996), 84.

[149] Dever, 136-137.

the apostles and the prophets.[150] In addition, all the community fellowship and all three treatises of Tertullian, Origen, and Cyprian allude to both private and communal prayers. As in the case of times, "everyplace is suitable for prayer" writes Origen. Tertullian makes a similar point, indicating prayer is essential for everyone, every day.[151] Just as important to the early church, we find dialogue concerning the Lord's Supper. There are inferences that "the Lord's Supper as a memorial is universally accepted. So it is not surprising that language is found frequently in the history of the Church, from Cyril of Jerusalem to John Chrysostom. Even Augustine frequently used such language."[152]

The Christian Middle Ages and the Age of the Reformation proved to be a time of transition and information. John Wycliffe was instrumental in providing believers the opportunity to study the Word daily. His action stressed the importance of every Christian being able to read and meditate on the Word of God through making the Bible available in the English language.[153]

---

[150] *Documents of the Christian Church,* Henry Bettenson and Chris Maunder, eds. (New York, NY: Oxford University Press, 1999), 72-73.

[151] Richard D. Stuckwisch, "Principles of Christian Prayer from the Third Century: A Brief Look at Origen, Tertullian and Cyprian With Some Comments on their Meaning Today," *Worship* 71, no.1 (Jan 1997): 2-19.

[152] Dever, 109.

[153] James P. Eckerman, *Exploring Church History* (Wheaton, IL: Crossway Books, 2002), 46.

The Reason We Stay Broken and Disconnected

Thomas Kempis, the author of *The Imitation of Christ* also wanted every believer to apply the spiritual disciplines of reading the Word and prayer. He tells his readers "Never is idle or vagrant be always reading or writing or praying or meditating, or employed in some useful labor for the common good."[154]

Ignatius Loyola proposed that union with God could be sought and found in the world among men through prayer. The necessity of formal prayer is pointed out in his *Spiritual Exercises*, where there is a whole series of meditations, contemplations, and vocal prayers required of his followers.[155] For the Church, there is a necessity for each individual to be reconciled to God and to each other. Ignatius believed that both prayer and action done according to God's will are basically two aspects of the same thing, the love of God.[156] Therefore, he wrote the *Spiritual Exercises* to provide guidance to Christians and to help them remain faithful. In this instruction, they were called to meditate on the Word, repent from the sin in their lives, and reflect on the death, burial, and resurrection of the Lord.[157]

---

[154] George A. Lane, *Christian Spirituality: an Historical Sketch* (Chicago, IL: Loyola University Press, 1984), 31.

[155] Ibid., 46-47.

[156] Lane, 55.

[157] Earle E. Cairns, *Christianity Through the Centuries: A History of the Christian Church* (Grand Rapids, MI: Zondervan Publishing House, 1996), 344.

Moving into the sixteenth century, Martin Bucer and the Reformed Church of Strasbourg practiced the psalms in daily prayer services. In addition to utilizing the psalms through worship and prayer, they also upheld scripture lessons. The use of the *Lectio continua* or Lectionary was applied for morning and evening prayer, reading through whole books of the Bible one at a time.[158] Martin Luther placed great emphasis on prayer and the necessity of Christians remaining connected to God through the practice of prayer. For Luther, "the sinful condition of the world which makes unbelief a constant reality for the Christian requires that he be constant in prayer."[159] Understanding the necessity of prayer, Luther goes further in his theology to express that prayer should be constant, spontaneous, and regulated. "As it is the business of tailors to make clothes and of cobblers to mend shoes, so it is the business of Christians to pray."[160] Therefore, affirming Christians continued to practice daily prayer through the reformation period. The Age of Reason, Revival, and Progress proves to engage in some noteworthy things in church history. Jeremy Taylor writes:

---

[158] Hughes Oliphant Old, "Daily prayer in the Reformed Church of Strasburg, 1525-1530" *Worship 52*, no. 2 (March 1978): 121-138.

[159] David P. Scaer, "Luther on Prayer," *Concordia Theological Quarterly*, 47, no. 4 (October 1983): 305-316.

[160] Donald S. Whitney, *Spiritual Disciplines For The Christian Life* (Colorado Springs, CO: Navpress, 1991), 64.

> In the Church of England we have the Word of God, the Faith of the Apostles, the Creeds of the Primitive Church, the Articles of the four first General Councils, a holy liturgy, excellent prayers, perfect Sacraments, faith and repentance, the Ten Commandments, and the sermons of Christ, and all the precepts and counsels of the Gospel. We teach the necessity of good works, and require and strictly exact the severity of holy life.[161]

In the 1700s, in his *Minutes of Several Conversations*, John Wesley discusses two classes of the "means of grace," namely, the instituted and the prudential, which are the two definitions of utmost importance when understanding the intended result of discipleship. They can also be identified as "works of piety and works of mercy."[162] In the instituted means of grace, "works of piety," we find the acts of prayer, searching the Scripture, the Lord's Supper, fasting, and the Christian Conference (i.e., accountability to others). Prudential means of grace or "works of mercy" are identified as:

---

[161] Bettenson, 298-299.

[162] Andrew C. Thompson, "John Wesley and the Means of Grace: Historical and Theological Context" (ThD diss., Duke Divinity School, 2012), 146-150.

> Means of grace, which are context-specific rules that help us, grow in grace. These will vary from person to person and from situation to situation, because what is effective in one context may not be effective in another. However, all Christians should see some evidence of growth when they attend to the following prudential means: self-scrutiny, self-denial, 'taking up our cross' (i.e. performing duties which are difficult or sacrificial), and 'exercise of the presence of God' (i.e. staying focused on God and remembering that He is watching us) we find that grace varies according to changing circumstances.[163]

Wesley further explains means of grace as "doing no harm, abstaining from swearing, drunkenness, smuggling, and extravagant dress, and useless diversion, self-indulgence, doing good, caring for the poor, with particular responsibility for Christians, and attending upon all ordinances of God."[164] All are evidence of prudential grace.

---

[163] Kevin Twain Lowery, "The Means of Grace: Wesley's Meditation between Naturalism and Mysticism" (2004) Faculty Scholarship Theology Paper 7. Available http://www.digitalcommonsolivet.edu/theo_facp/7 (accessed January 21, 2014).

[164] Bert Affleck, "John Wesley's spiritual disciplines for today's pastor," *Perkins Journal* 40, no.1 (January 1987): 1-8.

He was convinced that one should be dedicated to God fully or not at all. He and his brother formed "The Holy Club" in 1729, and the basic principles of this group were to meet together, to perform a daily self-examination, to have communion twice a week, and to engage in Bible study, penance, fasting, and works of mercy.[165] All in all, his practices are indicative of a person who strives to apply the spiritual disciples set forth in Act 2:42-47.

Through the 1700s and the early 1800s, James McGready, who was highly influenced by the works of Jonathan Edwards, began a movement in the mountains of Kentucky. There, his congregation fasted monthly and participated in weekly prayer. These revivals led to the observance of the Lord's Supper, which developed into what is now known as "the camp meeting." Camp meetings offered days and often weeks of gathering where Presbyterian, Baptist, and Methodist preachers proclaimed the Gospel to eager listeners.[166] The camp revivals brought people together to fast, pray, hear the Word of God, and gain a renewed motivation. In *Christianity Today*, A. W. Tozer proclaimed:

> We must face the fact that many today are notoriously careless in their living. This attitude finds its way into the church. We

---

[165] Robin Maas and Gabriel O'Donnell, *Spiritual Traditions for the Contemporary Church*. (Nashville, TN: Abingdon Press, 1990), 307.

[166] Eckerman, 87.

> have liberty, we have money, and we live in comparative luxury. As a result, discipline practically has disappeared. What would a violin solo sound like if the strings on the musician's instrument were all hanging loose, not stretched tight, not disciplined?[167]

In the early 1900s, Dietrich Bonhoeffer sums up his ideas of Christian community and fellowship as spiritual life together. He argues that life together "will remain sound and healthy only where it does not form itself into a movement [...] but rather where it understands itself as being part of the only, holy, Catholic, Christian Church, where it shares actively and passively in the sufferings and struggles and promise of the whole Church."[168] In his *Life Together*, Bonhoeffer suggests a close Christian community, which focuses on the disciplines of the Church. Meanwhile, Jenkins and McBride introduce a parallel thought on King and Bonhoeffer and their ideas on community embodying redemption. They presented the concept of combating social sin by the formation of "Christian Communities."[169]

---

[167] Whitney, 213.

[168] John Armstrong et al., *A Servant's Journal, 21 Articles on Reconciliation, Fellowship & The Grace of God* (New Lenox, IL: Leadership Resources, 1992), 57.

[169] Willis Jenkins and Jennifer M. McBride eds., *Bonhoeffer and King* (Minneapolis: Fortress Press, 2010), 164.

Martin Luther King felt reconciliation comes through as a worshiping community. This thought is summed up in the terms the "great world house" or the "worldwide neighborhood," which suggests a totally integrated human family, unconcerned with human differences and devoted to the ethical norms of love, justice, and community.[170]

William Barclay emphasized the need for spiritual disciplines when he stated, "nothing was ever achieved without discipline: and many an athlete and many a man has been ruined because he abandoned discipline and let himself grow slack."[171] J. I. Packer explains his concern that Christians should understand the term "fellowship." He wants to ensure that mere dinner or a church meeting is not mistaken for fellowship. To Packer, "fellowship is one of the greatest words of the New Testament: it denotes something vital to a Christian's spiritual health, and central to the true life of the church. It is of the first importance."[172]

The Age of Ideologies ignites great thought from the American theologian and Lutheran Evangelical, Marva Dawn. She discusses how the pastor and contemporary translator of the *Message Bible*, Eugene Peterson, and the people at Regent College in Vancouver, British Columbia, made her feel as family and welcomed her with no

---

[170] Jenkins, 239.

[171] Whitney, 20.

[172] Armstrong, 97.

pretenses. She goes on to state, "To build a community requires a wide diversity of efforts, including vigilance against envy or resentment, as well as the more positive labors of offering hospitality, engaging in conversation, and persisting in prayer for one another."[173] In her experiences, Marva Dawn indicates:

> Everyone is looking for love, for loyalty, for sure solution to the lonely yearning expressed in the questions 'To whom do I belong?' and 'Who can I trust?' Our churches offer the gift of genuine community that is trustworthy (and when it is not we offer confession and absolution) and the greatest gift of the truth about the totally reliable God to whom we all belong.[174]

Moving forward to the 1960s, the local church instruction has not shifted with the wind. Ligon Duncan, pastor of the Southern Presbyterian Church, gives instruction to the Church for the elements of church gatherings: "Read the Bible, preach the Bible, pray the Bible, sing the Bible,

---

[173] Marva Dawn and Eugene Peterson, *The Unnecessary Pastor: Rediscovering the Call* (Grand Rapids, MI: William B. Eerdmans Publishing Company, 2000), 221.

[174] Ibid., 218.

and see the Bible."[175] While Mark Dever of the Capitol Hill Baptist Church suggests the responsibilities of the church member in society as:

> Church members, like Christians, are to be baptized and regularly to attend the Lord's Supper. They are to hear God's Word and to obey it. They are regularly to fellowship for mutual edification. They are to love God, one another, and those outside their fellowship: and they are to evidence the fruit of the Spirit. They are to worship God in all the activities of their home, work, community, and life.[176]

In closing, it is evident that throughout history from the early makings of the Church to present day, spiritual disciplines are applicable in the life of the believer. We are called to reconcile with one another. Therefore, "forgiveness is necessary in every home because without it grudges build and become uncrossable walls, bitterness clogs up the soul."[177] It is also necessary for us to model the early church to study the Word, to fellowship with one another, to worship God, and to share our resources so that every

---

[175] Dever, 70.

[176] Ibid., 41.

[177] Ibid., 44.

need is met. In *Transformational Discipleship*, the authors lift the idea that a transformed disciple must begin with the study of the Word of God and continual prayer.[178]

Applying Theology to Life

In search of theological foundations for the problem of reconciling relationships through spiritual disciplines, the realm of possibilities all consistently fall under what is considered practical theology, which includes the interwoven theology of pastoral care, spiritual formation, congregational studies, and education. Through practical theology, one will be able to navigate through reconciling relationships. It is clear we are not just to hear what is right; we are to do what is right. In practical theology, we want to be able to take the knowledge, obtain it, live it, and embody it. The apostle Paul expounded this doctrine to inform his readers so that they might have more data. His intent was that the doctrine he expounded be applied to everyday life.[179] The crux of the problem in broken relationships can be solved by the application of various spiritual disciplines, more specifically, the disciplines found in the doctrine of the Church.

---

[178] Eric Geiger, Michael Kelly, and Philip Nation, *Transformational Discipleship: How People Really Grow* (Nashville, TN: B & H Publishing Group, 2012), 223.

[179] Millard Erickson, *Introducing Christian Doctrine* (Grand Rapids: Baker Book House, 1992), 16.

According to Klaus Penzel, pastoral and practical theology emerged almost from the beginning of church history.[180] Although, it is evident how these could have been considered as the same, it was necessary to separate the two, ensuring life application procedures. When we look at pastoral theology, we see there is a need to understand our condition prior to accepting Christ. Pastoral theology is defined as "the theological study of the Church's action in its own life and towards society, in response to the activity of God."[181] On the other hand, practical theology is defined as "critical and constructive reflection within a living community about human experience and interaction, involving a correlation of Christian story and other perspectives, leading to an interpretation of meaning and value, and resulting in everyday guidelines and skills for the formation of person and communities."[182]

As identified previously, many would still say that both pastoral and practical theologies are generally the same, or at least they overlap tremendously. Leroy Howe finds it difficult to separate practical theology from pastoral care.[183]

---

[180] Klaus Penzel, "Some thoughts on Schleiermacher and practical theology today," *Perkins Journal* 35, no. 3 (Summer 1982): 1-7.

[181] Woodward, 24.

[182] James N. Poling and Donald E. Miller, *Foundations for a Practical Theology of Ministry* (Nashville, TN: Abington Press, 2000), 62.

[183] Howe, "Beginnings in Practical Theology: An Account of a Journey," *Perkins Journal 35, no. 3 (Summer 1982)*, 22-27. ALTA Religion Database with ATLASerials EBSCO Host (accessed December 12, 2012).

Successful pastoral care is lived out through the minister, thus providing a model to all who are in the care of the pastor. Arguments of difference are just as creditable. The greater concern, according to Ray Anderson, is that most have a handle on systematic theology, but have no grasp of practical theology. He states, "the core theology of the Bible, both Old Testament and New Testament, is practical theology before it becomes systematic theology,"[184] as long as we take into consideration that when practicing, teaching, leading, and mending we go beyond information dissemination of preaching, teaching, and counseling, and provide applicable solutions with simple outcomes.

"Pastoral/practical theology is a place where religious belief, tradition, and practice meets contemporary experiences, questions and actions; and conducts a dialogue that is mutually enriching, intellectually critical, and practically transforming."[185] People are given opportunity to move beyond thinking reconciliation, and even speaking the words of forgiveness, to actually doing what it takes to mend relationships. The process of effectively reconciling relationships must begin with the Church. In his work, *Transforming Practice*, E. L. Graham states:

> There is still considerable disagreement about appropriate terminology, 'practical'

---

[184]Ray S. Anderson, *The Shape of Practical Theology: Empowering Ministry with Theological Praxis* (Downers Grove: IVP Academic, 2001), 14.

[185]Woodward, 7.

denoting the generic activities of Christian ministry and 'pastoral' the more interpersonal levels of care. I am increasingly moved to favor 'practical theology', given my emphasis on the discipline as the study of Christian practice, and to locate pastoral theology as one of a number of practical theologies, but distinguished by its focus on the theory of practice of the human life cycle.[186]

Practical theology evolved from the New Testament writings of Paul, as well as the early discourse of Augustine. There have been many different contributors to the development of practical theology, such as Chrysostom, Gregory of Nazianzus, Gregory the Great, Martin Luther, Duns Scotus, Andreas Hyperius, and Gisbert Voetius to name a few. Practical theology appeared in the work of Austrian Gisbert Voetius, who saw it "consisting of moral theology, ascetic theology (reflection on devotion), and ecclesial polity (reflection on preaching, catechesis, etc.)."[187] However, practical theology evolved in the thoughts of a German theologian, Friedrich Schleiermacher, who

---

[186]Elaine Graham, *The Blackwell Reader in Pastoral and Practical Theology,* eds. James Woodward and Stephen Pattison (Malden, MA: Blackwell Publishers, 2000), 114.

[187]Andrew Root, "Practical Theology: That Is It and How Does It Work," *Journal of Youth Ministry* 7, no. 2 (May 2009): 55-72.

viewed practical theology as an enterprise primarily for the Church, itself conceived as a community of believers.[188] In his *Brief Outline on the Study of Theology*, Friedrich Schleiermacher describes the "scientific" contribution of theology along the lines of modern discipline. Also, in his theological encyclopedias, "four disciplines became standard: biblical studies, church history, systematic theology, and practical theology."[189] Although, it may be said that Schleiermacher is not the father of practical theology, he was the first to constitute it as an academic discipline in a theological faculty.[190] Schleiermacher argued that practical theology was an essential element. Practical theology revolves around two axes: (1) the critical method used to bring together the various interpretations available in the Christian tradition and culture, and (2) the relationship between church and society.[191]

James Poling claims that the terms "critical" and "constructive" are borrowed terms, in that practical theology is more than awareness of analytical methods of socio-historical research. It also must include constructive affirmations that involve descriptive and normative elements. Therefore, it is determined by Poling and Miller that

---

[188] Howe, 22-27.

[189] Kapic, 327.

[190] Penzel, 1-7.

[191] Poling, 14-41.

> Practical theology is reflection, which means that it is not the same as lived experience. Practical theology is a form of discipline, thought about, an experience which is an abstraction from community interaction. Thus, it is not whatever community does in its life together. Rather, it is a form of thinking about life. Its purpose is to clarify perceptions about the structures and tendencies of experience, but it is always less than full experience and must be tested within experience frequently to verify and correct its claims.[192]

James Fowler adds that practical theology aims to aid the Church in being theologically discerning. Practical theology aims to frame and generate a language for sharing of the ethical and spiritual riches—and imperatives—of Christian faith in public while addressing the issues that threaten the common good.[193]

In his *Church Dogmatic*, Karl Barth informs the reader that "freedom under the Word implies the assumption of responsibility by all members of the Church for the

---

[192] Poling, 63.

[193] James W. Fowler, "Practical Theology and Theological Education: Some Models and Questions." *Theology Today* 42, no. 1 (April 1985): 43-58.

interpretation and application of the Holy Scriptures."[194] Influenced by the thought process of Barth, Dietrich Bonhoeffer says that "one of the main reasons why readers find Bonhoeffer's writings so compelling lies in the inner strength and intensity of his relationship with Jesus Christ developed in the practical everyday life of a Christian community."[195] Bonhoeffer, who describes a simple life in common with believers includes "a daily schedule of prayer, meditation, mutual encouragement, common studies, and worship together"[196] also insisting on "the practical application daily, morning and evening prayer, communal worship which encompassed singing, reading scripture and prayer."[197]

Since humanity should exist in community, T. S. Eliot said, "There is no life that is not in community. And no community not lived in praise of God."[198] Scripture begins and ends with God calling humanity into relationship

---

[194] James C. Livingston, Francis Schussler Fiorenza, with Sarah Coakley and James H. Evans, Jr., *Modern Christian Thought: The Twentieth Century* (Minneapolis, MN: 2006), 105.

[195] Geffrey B. Kelly and F. Burton Nelson, *The Cost of Moral Leadership* (Grand Rapid, MI: William B. Eerdmans Publishing Company, 2003), 145.

[196] Ibid., 157.

[197] Ibid., 162.

[198] T. S. Eliot, "Choruses from 'The Rock,'" *Complete Poems and Plays* (New York, NY: Harcourt and Brace, 1952), 101.

with the divine community and with one another.[199] This concept may be considered a process of practical theology, which works well in a community when done continually and consistently. Practical theology of care, according to Don S. Browning,

> Should be seen as the theology of the human life cycle, both what this cycle should be when conceived normatively and what should be done to restore it when its development has been arrested or in some way gone astray. A practical theology of care should deal with what the church does in shaping lives, not only those of its own members, but the lives of individuals in society at large.[200]

The reality of community lies in our mere understanding and practicing of the basic principles outlined in

---

[199] Gareth Weldon Icenogle, *Biblical Foundations for Small Group Ministry: An Integrative Approach* (Downers Grove, IL: InterVarsity Press, 1993) under chap. 1, sec. "God's Call To Small Group Community," Logos Bible Software.

[200] Don S. Browning 1981, "Toward a Practical Ttheology of Care," *Union Seminary Quarterly Review 36, no. 2-3* (Winter 1981): *159-172*.

the Christian faith. It was Dietrich Bonhoeffer who said, "Christianity means community through Jesus Christ."[201]

To be followers of Christ means we are all part of the body, which we call the Church. When approaching this concept of practical theology, it is necessary to realize that theology is something lived and experienced in a particular community.[202] Adele Ahlberg Calhoun, writer of *Spiritual Disciplines Handbook: Practices That Transform Us*, encourages practice in community. She goes on to explain that spiritual disciplines are to be learned in and through relationships.[203] It is in the community that people are afforded the opportunity to live out a theology. Anderson goes on to describe that the discipline of practical theology, by explaining human beings, are two sided.

> Human beings are participants as well as observers, worshipers as well as workers, and all of these aspects are potential sources of theological knowledge. As Stephen Pattison astutely observes, 'Only in action can the meaning of love and compassion

---

[201] James H. Harris, *Pastoral Theology* (Minneapolis, MN: Fortress Press, 1991), 29.

[202] Ray S. Anderson, *The Shape of Practical Theology: Empowering Ministry with Theological Praxis* (Downers Grove: IVP Academic, 2001), 22.

[203] Adele Ahlberg Calhoun, *Spiritual Disciplines Handbook: Practices That Transform Us* (Downers Grove, IL: IVP Books, 2005), 21.

be revealed. Critical, analytical thinking is important, but it is not omniscient.'[204]

In review, it could be understood there is practical theology within the community, and it is worked out in the various interactions in the community. When we look at the purpose of practical theology, we revert to what Ray S. Anderson says, "the primary purpose of practical theology is to ensure that the church's public proclamation and Praxis in the world faithfully reflects the nature and purpose of God's continuing mission to the world, and in so doing, authentically addresses the contemporary context into which the church seeks to minister."[205] The Church as a community is a model to all who see its reflection. This is what Stanley Hauerwas claims when he says it is not the first task of the Church to go out and change the world. Rather, the first task "is to become itself, plainly enough for the world to see that there exists a new creation."[206] The Church must interact with the disciplines to reflect the Christ. Consequently the task of practical theology is to find more adequate ways of articulating the depth, richness, and possibility of life as they are found in concrete communities.[207]

---

[204] Anderson, 22.

[205] Marvin A. McMickle, *Caring Pastors, Caring People: Equipping Your Church for Pastoral Care* (Valley Forge, PA: Judson Press, 2011), 55-56.

[206] Susanne Johnson, *Christian Spiritual Formation: in the Church and Classroom* (Nashville, TN: Abington Press, 1989), 48.

[207] Poling, 64.

The use of practical theology goes hand-in-hand with the specific spiritual disciplines found in the New Testament, which will allow the believer to move forward in growth. The most important task of the Christian leader is to equip the believer. In *The Spirit of the Disciplines*, Dallas Willard indicates the need for believers to work toward acting naturally, and cites Dr. William C. De Vries, who said, "The reason you practice so much is so that you will do things automatically the same way every time."[208] Spiritual disciplines can unfold to be several different practices. In his book *Celebration of Discipline: The Path to Spiritual Growth*, Richard Foster indicates how "God intends the Disciplines of the spiritual life to be for ordinary human beings: people who have jobs, who care for children, who wash dishes and mow lawns."[209] Foster helps us to move from practical theology, beyond pastoral theology, to discussing spiritual formation, congregational studies, and Christian education.

Practical theology is further expanded through Christian education or the process of making disciples. It is important to look briefly at this subject as we move forward and solidify vastness of practical theology. "Education is the act or process of developing and cultivating mentally and morally,"[210] and is known as "the science dealing with the principles

---

[208] Willard, 153.

[209] Foster, 1.

[210] Charles A. Tidwell, *The Educational Ministry of a Church: A Comprehensive Models for Students and Ministers* (Nashville, TN: Broadman & Holman Publishers, 1996), 2.

and practices of teaching, training, disciplining, or forming."[211] When speaking of Christian education the Scriptures are the base, the foundation, the starting point, and the ending point. James Marion Frost, concerning education, said "The work of Sunday School is threefold: first, teach the Scriptures: second, teach the Scriptures: third, teach the Scriptures."[212] In essence, Christian education is not limited to Sunday school. It is so much more. The concept of preaching and teaching is central in the Bible and moves forward. "Christian education is the teaching function of the church. It can be understood only within the context of the church. It has validity only if the church is a nurturing community."[213]

Donald Rogers believes "religious education involves three dimensions: the work of opening people's eyes to see God's activity, helping them find ways to join in this activity in the world, and pointing to this activity so that others may see and receive the invitation to be partners with God."[214] In *Contemporary Approaches Christian Education,* Jack Seymour and Donald Miller state that there are at least five ways to approach Christian Education: "religious education, faith community, spiritual development, liberation, and

---

[211] Ibid., 2.

[212] Ibid., 80.

[213] Eleanor Daniel, John Wade, and Charles Gresham, *Introduction to Christian Education* (Cincinnati, OH: Standard Publishing, 1980), 22.

[214] Donald B. Rogers, *Urban Church Education* (Birmingham, AL: Religious Education Press, 1989), 31.

interpretation."²¹⁵ When you examine the many approaches, you find the process of Christian education is broad and deep. This is why Karen Tye, in the *Basics of Christian Education,* indicates that the shape or definition of Christian education may vary depending on the definer.²¹⁶ Therefore, in lieu of offering her own definition, she lends to the definition of Daniel Aleshire who states:

> Christian education involves those tasks and expressions of ministry that enable people (1) to learn the Christian story, both ancient and present; (2) to develop the skills they need to act out their faith: (3) to reflect on that story in order to live self-aware to its truth; and (4) to nurture the sensitivities they need to live together as a covenant community.²¹⁷

Jack Seymour looks at several approaches to Christian education by Daniel Schipani, Robert O'Gorman, Maria Harris, and Elizabeth Caldwell. In each approach, there

---

²¹⁵ Jack L. Seymour and Donald E. Miller, *Contemporary Approaches Christian Education* (Nashville, TN: Abington Press, 1982), 16.

²¹⁶ Karen B. Tye, *Basics of Christian Education* (St. Louis, MO: Chalice Press, 2000), 54.

²¹⁷ Daniel Aleshire, *Christian Education and Theology* in Christian Education Handbook, rev. ed., ed. Bruce P. Powers (Nashville, TN: Broadman and Holman, 1996), 13-28.

is a presumed connection and distinction. On the topic of social transformation, Daniel Schipani says, "transformation becomes both the goal and the process of education."[218] Robert O'Gorman, with a focus on faith community, states, "Learning the faith occurs as we participate in a faith community that seeks to promote authentic human development, that is, which enhances the relationship of persons to others, communities, and the cosmos."[219] In contrast, Maria Harris and Gabriel Moran, with their emphasis on spiritual development, believe "the ultimate goal of spiritual development is calling persons into relationship, friendship, care, and justice with others and the creation, the starting point for education is the person."[220] Finally, attentive to religious instruction, Elizabeth Caldwell "describes a formal process of theological reflection of teaching and learning, where we come to know, interpret, and incarnate the faith."[221]

In the opinion of the writer, an overflow of practical theology has led to congregational studies, which have slowly emerged as an important factor in practical theology. In *Leading Congregational Change*, the authors provide a discourse which infers that the driving force of

---

[218] Jack L Seymour, *Mapping Christian Education: Approaches to Congregational Learning* (Nashville, TN: Abingdon Press, 1997), 19.

[219] Ibid., 19.

[220] Ibid., 20.

[221] Ibid., 20.

congregational change is a strong spiritual (love God) and relational (love our neighbor) vitality.[222] Additionally, it is understood from their book that most of their hypothesis determines that reading the Book of Acts and continual study of the Word of God is essential. "Spiritual and relational vitality are the life-giving power that faithful people experience together as they passionately pursue God's vision for their lives."[223] In order for change to happen, the authors propose three stages: (1) making personal preparation, (2) creating urgency, and (3) establishing the vision community.[224]

As the congregation works through change, one of the actions suggested is to practice spiritual disciplines. The leadership and congregation need to spend "significant, consistent time seeking God's direction–through prayer, Bible study, meditation, solitude, and fasting."[225]

In addition to Christian education and congregational study, spiritual formation is a dynamic to practical theology, and should be utilized throughout this study. So what is spiritual formation? "Spiritual formation is the progressive patterning of a person's inner and outer life according to the image of Christ through

---

[222] Jim Herrington, Mike Bonem, and James H. Furr, *Leading Congregational Change: A Practical Guide for the Transformational Journey* (San Francisco: CA, 2000), 16-17.

[223] Ibid., 16.

[224] Ibid., 29-31.

[225] Ibid., 30.

intentional means of spiritual growth."[226] In her book *Artisanal Theology*, Lisa Hess states that formation "simply refers to that shaping–and–being–shaped experienced by real people living their lives within intimate and broader socio-cultural environments."[227] M. Robert Mulholland, Jr. "develops a fourfold definition of spiritual formation as (1) a process (2) of being conformed (3) to the image of Christ (4) for the sake of others."[228] Mulholland points out that nothing happens overnight, and just as physical birth starts in infancy, and it takes time to become a full grown adult, so does spiritual growth. Spiritual formation has also been confirmed, as indicated by Mulholland, who states, "it militates against our very mode of being and way of life"[229] because it removes our control and relies on God no matter how long it takes.

We are to conform into the image of Christ. This process of conformation into Christ's image is all for the sake of others. "Everything that God has done, is doing and ever will do in our lives to conform us to the image of Christ (which is the image of our wholeness) is not so that we may someday be set in a display case in heaven as

---

[226] Mel Lawrenz, *The Dynamics of Spiritual Formation* (Grand Rapids, MI: Baker Group, 2000), 15.

[227] Lisa M. Hess, *Artisanal Theology: Intentional Formation in Radically Conventional Companionship* (Eugene, OR: Cascade Books, 2009), 5.

[228] M. Robert Mulholland, Jr., *Invitation To A Journey: A Road Map for Spiritual Formation* (Downers Grove, IL: Intervarsity Press, 1993), 15.

[229] Ibid., 30.

trophies of grace."[230] Everything that is happening in our lives should allow the glory of God to be made evident in our lives. Wilhoit states that formation is the job of the Church, and its whole existence is to form.[231] He goes on to say, "Christian formation refers to the intentional communal process of growing in our relationship with God and becoming conformed to Christ through the power of the Holy Spirit."[232] Therefore, practical theology in the forms of Christian education, congregational studies, and spiritual formation will be applicable in reconciling relationships through spiritual disciplines.

---

[230] Ibid., 40.

[231] Wilhoit, 15.

[232] Ibid., 23.

In the pews, we find all kinds of people. On any given Sunday, the preacher could be looking out at oppressors, exploiters, aggressors, invaders, abusers, rapists, murderers, and more. At the same time, however, the preacher is likely to be confronted with the victims of these sins so that those who have been oppressed, exploited, injured, invaded, abused, raped, and bereft—as well as their families and friends—are also there, waiting to hear a word from God.
-Andrew Sung Park "From Hurt to Healing"

Chapter Three

There is a Method to the Madness

NOW THAT THE foundations have been laid, we need to apply this method of reconciling relationships to our lives. This model will provide a tool to help individuals who have partnered together develop concrete and effective habits for reconciling relationships by maneuvering through the process of forgiveness and the application of specific spiritual disciplines. The process will be through the means of practical application or practical theology.

In order to properly apply this model, individuals must commit to partner with at least one person and spend personal time in reflection and study. "The goals of human development have always included the concepts of independence, freedom, autonomy, empowerment, and self-direction; and therefore these concepts should be a major part of educating adults."[233] Objectively, following this model should also identify factors contributing

---

[233] Patricia Cranton, *Professional Development as Transformative Learning: New Perspectives for Teachers of Adults* (San Francisco, CA: Jossey-Bass Publishers 1996), 50.

to broken or disconnected families and severed relationships, examine the impact of applying spiritual disciplines when applying them in the reconciliation process, establish trust in God and the promises outlined in the Bible, and obtain skills for everyday Christian living. Through the process of action research, this study should "effect change or action which involves improving the quality of life of the individuals involved."[234]

The writer submits that most believers do not automatically move into a growth process or understand the necessity of applying spiritual disciplines. Although there is a desire for change, it is necessary to be in an environment that promotes that change. Without such an environment to foster communication and application of the various spiritual disciplines, new and even long time converts may remain non-productive or inactive members. A major barrier or distraction to Christian growth and involvement is the inability to reconcile and move forward into productive relationships, especially within the family and the Church. This happens for various reasons and can be remedied when individuals understand the process of reconciliation by spending time in the Word, in prayer or worship, and in fellowship.

Once you apply this model, it will examine your relationships and then impact and transformation all of the

---

[234] Davydd. J. Greenwood & Morten Levin, *Introduction to Action Research: Social Research for Social Change* (Thousand Oaks, CA: SAGE Publications Inc., 1998), 4.

individuals within your study circle. The methodology utilized in this model by the writer will involve reconciling family relationships through spiritual disciplines. Take the time necessary to follow the six devotionals, praise the God of reconciliation, meditate on God's revelation, and communicate with God through prayer. Reconciliation will follow.

Devotion and Dialogue

All devotionals will include aspects of reconciliation, the Word of God, breaking of bread, fellowship, and prayer. This model will provide a confidential environment where participants are able to recognize and articulate brokenness. It will also provide a safe environment where participants can apply the skills of reconciliation, and thereby experience healing by interacting with the spiritual disciplines. Participants will move toward becoming effective change agents in their relationships. The following objectives have been established for this model: (1) to identify factors contributing to broken or disconnected family and severed relationships, (2) to examine the impact of applying spiritual disciplines to the reconciliation process, (3) to establish trust in God and the promises outlined in the Bible, and (4) to obtain skills for everyday Christian living.

This is a disclaimer: make sure you complete this section with at least one individual. Please resist the temptation to take this walk alone. Please resist the temptation not to sing the praise song. Sing it even if you do not know the melody. Make it up if you have to. It will provide intentional time with you and the Lord. Don't just read the scripture, but discuss the scripture and talk through the questions. I say again read every scripture and pray at the end of each devotional. Remember to take time out to eat a meal with your partner(s) in this endeavor. The ingredients of this model are: (1) the Word of God, (2) a Meal, (3) Prayer, and (4) Praise. Complete these devotional sessions in six days, six weeks, or six months. It does not matter how you slice it. Just complete it!

DAY I – I Surrender All

All to Jesus I surrender, All to Him I freely give;
I will ever love and trust Him, In His presence daily live.

> I surrender all,
> I surrender all.
> All to Thee, my blessed Savior,
> I surrender all.

All to Jesus I surrender, humbly at His feet I bow,
Worldly pleasures all forsaken; Take me, Jesus,
take me now.

All to Jesus I surrender, Make me, Savior, wholly Thine;
Let me feel Thy Holy Spirit, Truly know that
Thou art mine.

All to Jesus I surrender, Lord, I give myself to Thee;
Fill me with Thy love and power, Let Thy blessing
fall on me.

All to Jesus I surrender, now I feel the sacred flame.
Oh, the joy of full salvation! Glory, glory to His name![235]

Scripture Reading

Genesis 50:19-20

> But Joseph said to them, "Don't be afraid. Am I in the place of God? You intended to harm me, but God intended it for good to accomplish what is now being done, the saving of many lives."[236]

Psalm 34:8

> O taste and see that the LORD is good; happy are those who take refuge in him.

---

[235] Hymnal.net Source, *I Surrender All.* http://www.hymnal.net/en/hymn/h/441#ixzz314CWcw7Q [accessed May 8, 2014]

[236] Genesis 50:19-20 (New Revised Standard Version). Unless otherwise indicated, the New Revised Standard Version will be used throughout this chapter.

DAY I – I Surrender All

Reflection through the Word

1. We are not in control of our lives, God is.

    - Genesis 30:2 Jacob became very angry with Rachel and said, "Am I in the place of God, who has withheld from you the fruit of the womb?"
    - Proverbs 19:21 The human mind may devise many plans, but it is the purpose of the Lord that will be established.
    - Matthew 19:26 But Jesus looked at them and said, "For mortals it is impossible, but for God all things are possible."
    - Ephesians 1:11 In Christ we have also obtained an inheritance, having been destined according to the purpose of him who accomplishes all things according to his counsel and will.

2. Vengeance is not ours, it's the Lord's.

    - Leviticus 19:18 You shall not take vengeance or bear a grudge against any of your people, but you shall love your neighbor as yourself: I am the Lord.
    - Numbers 23:19 God is not a human being, that he should lie, or a mortal, that he should change his mind. Has he promised, and will

he not do it? Has he spoken, and will he not fulfill it?
- Deuteronomy 32:35 Vengeance is mine, and recompense, for the time when their foot shall slip; because the day of their calamity is at hand, their doom comes swiftly.
- Romans 12:19 Beloved, never avenge yourselves, but leave room for the wrath of God; for it is written, "Vengeance is mine, I will repay, says the Lord."

3. Transferring what was meant for evil to good.

- Proverbs 16:9 The human mind plans the way, but the LORD directs the steps.
- Isaiah 54:17 No weapon that is fashioned against you shall prosper, and you shall confute every tongue that rises against you in judgment. This is the heritage of the servants of the LORD and their vindication from me, says the LORD.
- Jeremiah 29:11 For surely I know the plans I have for you, says the LORD, plans for your welfare and not for harm, to give you a future with hope.
- Romans 8:28 we know that all things work together for good for those who love God, who are called according to his purpose.

DAY 1 – I Surrender All

Notes

We can look at what God has done only with humility, anticipating that God will constantly reveal to us new dimensions of the acts of significance. As Philip Yancey summarizes from his interviews with Frederick Buechner, the latter profoundly trusts that God is alive and present in the world, but he is not at all surprised that God gives us only momentary glimpses into a mystery of such depth, power, and beauty that if we were to see it head on, in any way other than in glimpses, I suspect we would be annihilated.[237]

Questions to Ponder

- What does it mean to surrender?
- What does surrender mean, according to the Joseph narrative?
- Who is in control? Did the scripture lesson teach you any new information about who is in control of your life?
- Is vengeance ours? Have you taken matters into your own hands in past relationships?
- Do you now have greater belief that everything works for our good?

---

[237] Marva Dawn, *Talking the Walk: Letting Christian Language Live Again* (Grand Rapids: MI: Brazos Press, 2005), 107.

Application

How will you apply what you have learned today?

1.

2.

3.

Closing Prayer

Lord... [Spend time in prayer to God concerning your desire to surrender.]

Thank God in advance. Amen.

DAY 11 – Change My Heart, Part 1

Change my heart oh God, Make it ever true.
Change my heart oh God, May I be like you.
You are the potter, I am the clay,
Mold me and make me, and this is what I pray.[238]

Scripture Reading

Genesis 50:15-18

Realizing that their father was dead, Joseph's brothers said, "What if Joseph still bears a grudge against us and pays us back in full for all the wrong that we did to him?" So they approached Joseph, saying, "Your father gave this instruction before he died, 'Say to Joseph: I beg you, forgive the crime of your brothers and the wrong they did in harming you.' Now therefore please forgive the crime of the servants of the God of your father." Joseph wept when they spoke to him. Then his brothers also wept, fell down before him, and said, "We are here as your slaves."

---

[238] Vineyard, *Change My Heart,* http://www.lyricsmode.com/lyrics/v/vineyard/change_my_heart_oh_god.html (accessed, May 9, 2014).

It's About Relationships

<u>Matthew 6:14</u>

For if you forgive others their trespasses, your heavenly Father will also forgive you.

Reflections through the Word

1. Look at attitudes and circumstances.

   - What attitude did Joseph's brothers harbor against him?
   - What caused them to have this attitude?

     o <u>Genesis 37:4</u> But when his brothers saw that their father loved him more than all his brothers, they hated him, and could not speak peaceably to him.

   - What are some of the mitigating circumstances that have caused separation in your relationships?
   - How did this attitude manifest itself?

     o <u>Genesis 37:18-20</u> But they saw him from a distance, and before he came near to them, they conspired to kill him. They said to one another, "Here comes this dreamer. Come now, let us kill him and throw him into one of the pits; then we shall say that a wild animal has devoured him, and we shall see what will become of his dreams."

o <u>Genesis 37:26-27</u> Then Judah said to his brothers, "What profit is it if we kill our brother and conceal his blood? Come, let us sell him to the Ishmaelite's, and not lay our hands on him, for he is our brother, our own flesh." And his brothers agreed.

- What type of attitudes manifested in your various relationships?

2. Forgiveness Unfolded

    a. When we forgive

        - <u>Luke 7:41-42</u> "A certain creditor had two debtors; one owed five hundred denarii, and the other fifty. When they could not pay, he canceled the debts for both of them. Now which of them will love him more?"

    b. Settling the debt

        - <u>Matthew 5:38-39</u> "You have heard that it was said, 'An eye for an eye and a tooth for a tooth.' But I say to you, do not resist an evildoer. But if anyone strikes you on the right cheek, turn the other also.

Notes

DAY II – Change My Heart, Part 1

Questions to Ponder

- How would you explain forgiveness?
- What caused the brothers to confess and beg for forgiveness?
- What feelings have caused you to move to asking for forgiveness?
- Define "grudge" in your own words.
- Are the brothers reflecting how they believe Joseph feels about them or how they felt about Joseph?
- Is there any guilt you may be still harboring?
- Was their fear irrational?

    o <u>Genesis 27:41</u> Now Esau hated Jacob because of the blessing with which his father had blessed him, and Esau said to himself, "The days of mourning for my father are approaching; then I will kill my brother Jacob."

- What does this say about the brothers?
- Did they actually forgive their brother?
- Do you believe the brothers were able to rid themselves of the sense of guilt incurred when Joseph was still a boy?

Gandhi said, "An eye for an eye, a tooth for a tooth cannot sustain itself forever; ultimately both parties end up blind and toothless."[239]

Application

How will you apply what you have learned today?

1.

2.

3.

Closing Prayer

Lord… [Spend time in prayer asking God for a change of heart.]
Thank God in advance. Amen.

---

[239] Robert Jeffress, *When Forgiveness Doesn't Make Sense* (Colorado Springs, CO: Waterbrook Press, 2000), 52.

DAY III - Change My Heart, Part 2

Lord, prepare me to be a sanctuary,
Pure and holy, tried and true;
With thanksgiving, I'll be a living
Sanctuary for You. [240]

Scripture Reading

Genesis 50:15-18

Realizing that their father was dead, Joseph's brothers said, "What if Joseph still bears a grudge against us and pays us back in full for all the wrong that we did to him?" So they approached Joseph, saying, "Your father gave this instruction before he died, 'Say to Joseph: I beg you, forgive the crime of your brothers and the wrong they did in harming you.' Now therefore please forgive the crime of the servants of the God of your father." Joseph wept when they spoke to him. Then his brothers also wept, fell down before him, and said, "We are here as your slaves."

---

[240] Vineyard, *Sanctuary,* http://www.lyricsmode.com/lyrics/v/vineyard/sanctuary.html (accessed May 9, 2014).

Matthew 6:14

For if you forgive others their trespasses, your heavenly Father will also forgive you.

Lesson: Change My Heart

Reflection through the Word

1. A Second Look at Forgiveness

    a. Reflecting on Joseph's Brothers Petition

    - What information did the brother's note contain?
    - How are we able to rise above personal revenge?

        o Luke 23:34 Then Jesus said, "Father, forgive them; for they do not know what they are doing." And they cast lots to divide his clothing.

        o Matthew 18:21-22 Then Peter came and said to him, "Lord, if another member of the church sins against me, how often should I forgive? As many as seven times?" Jesus said to him, "Not

DAY III - Change My Heart, Part 2

> seven times, but, I tell you, seventy-seven times.
> - Luke 17:3-4 Be on your guard! If another disciple sins, you must rebuke the offender, and if there is repentance, you must forgive. And if the same person sins against you seven times a day, and turns back to you seven times and says, 'I repent,' you must forgive."
> - Ephesians 4:32 and be kind to one another, tenderhearted, forgiving one another, as God in Christ has forgiven you.

2. Define "reconciliation" in your own words.

    a. <u>Matthew 5:23-24</u> So when you are offering your gift at the altar, if you remember that your brother or sister has something against you, leave your gift there before the altar and go; first be reconciled to your brother or sister, and then come and offer your gift.
    b. <u>2 Corinthians 5:18</u> All this is from God, who reconciled us to himself through Christ, and has given us the ministry of reconciliation.

C. S. Lewis said, "Forgiveness is a beautiful word, until you have something to forgive."[241]

Dr. W. A. Criswell said, "If I ever fall into sin, I pray that I don't fall into the hands of those censorious, critical, self-righteous judges in the church. I'd rather fall into the hands of the barkeepers, streetwalkers, and dope peddlers, because the church people tend to tear each other apart with their gossipy tongues."[242]

3. Is forgetting reasonable?

   a. <u>Jeremiah 31:34</u> No longer shall they teach one another, or say to each other, "Know the LORD," for they shall all know me, from the least of them to the greatest, says the LORD; for I will forgive their iniquity, and remember their sin no more.

Dr. Church Lynch says, "All memories are stored in the brain by electronic impulses and by chemical transference. Messages are sent simultaneously from nerve to nerve both electronically and chemically. Memory is not a spiritual function it's a biological function. Our brain can store at least six hundred memories a second. That would work out to about one-and-a-half trillion bits of

---

[241] Robert Jeffress, *When Forgiveness Doesn't Make Sense* (Colorado Springs, CO: Waterbrook Press, 2000), 9.

[242] Ibid., 13.

information if we were to live seventy-five years. That is awesome when I consider that I don't even remember what I had for breakfast two days ago."[243]

    b. Remembering who God is and who we are helps us to forgive.

        1) <u>Psalm 107:1</u> O gives thanks to the LORD, for he is good; for his steadfast love endures forever.

        2) <u>Exodus 33:19</u> And he said, "I will make all my goodness pass before you, and will proclaim before you the name, 'The LORD'; and I will be gracious to whom I will be gracious, and will show mercy on whom I will show mercy.

        3) <u>Romans 5:8</u> But God proves his love for us in that while we still were sinners Christ died for us.

        4) <u>1 John 4:8-10</u> Whoever does not love does not know God, for God is love. God's love was revealed among us in this way: God sent his only Son into the world so that we might live through him. In this is love, not that we loved God, but that he loved us

---

[243] Chuck Lynch, *I Should Forget But: Finding Release From Anger and Bitterness* (Nashville, TN: Word Publishing, 1998), 27.

and sent his Son to be the atoning sacrifice for our sins.

5) <u>Romans 12:3</u> For by the grace given to me I say to everyone among you not to think of yourself more highly than you ought to think, but to think with sober judgment, each according to the measure of faith that God has assigned.

6) <u>Titus 3:5</u> He saved us, not because of any works of righteousness that we had done, but according to his mercy, through the water of rebirth and renewal by the Holy Spirit.

c. Someone has to pay for sin to be forgiven and for relationships to be reconciled.

1) <u>Isaiah 53:6</u> All we like sheep have gone astray; we have all turned to our own way, and the LORD has laid on him the iniquity of us all.

2) <u>Psalm 103:12</u> As far as the east is from the west, so far he removes our transgressions from us.

3) <u>John 1:29</u> The next day he saw Jesus coming toward him and declared, "Here is the Lamb of God who takes away the sin of the world!

DAY III - Change My Heart, Part 2

4) <u>2 Corinthians 5:19</u> That is, in Christ God was reconciling the world to himself, not counting their trespasses against them, and entrusting the message of reconciliation to us.

5) <u>Colossians 1:13-14</u> He has rescued us from the power of darkness and transferred us into the kingdom of his beloved Son, in whom we have redemption, the forgiveness of sins.

Notes

Questions to Ponder

- Do you have people and situations in your life that are hard to get past?
- Are there areas of bitterness in your life?
- Are there times when you do things out of anger?
- What kind of things?
- We should walk in forgiveness. How do we do that?
- Have there been instances in your life when someone clearly meant evil against you?
- Have you seen, in retrospect, God working those events for your good and His glory? In what ways?
- Have you been able to forgive all your offenders as Joseph forgave his brothers?
- Is there, perhaps, an appropriate way for you to let that person know he or she is forgiven?
- Why do we carry the sin Jesus already removed?
- Do you believe forgiveness is the pathway to reconciliation? Why?

DAY III - Change My Heart, Part 2

Application

How will you apply what you have learned today?

1.

2.

3.

Closing Prayer

Lord... [Spend time in prayer asking God to forgive you and help you to forgive others.]
Thank God in advance. Amen.

DAY IV - Give Me a Clean Heart

Give me a clean heart so I may serve Thee.
Lord, fix my heart so that I may be used by Thee.
For I'm not worthy of all these blessings.
Give me a clean heart, and I'll follow Thee.[244]

Scripture Reading

<u>Acts 2:42-47</u>

They devoted themselves to the apostles' teaching and fellowship, to the breaking of bread and the prayers. Awe came upon everyone, because many wonders and signs were being done by the apostles. All who believed were together and had all things in common; they would sell their possessions and goods and distribute the proceeds to all, as any had need. Day by day, as they spent much time together in the temple, they broke bread at home

---

[244] Ensemble Management, *Give Me a Clean Heart*, http://ensemblemgmt.com/pages/lyrics/GiveMeACleanHeart.html (accessed May 9, 2014).

and ate their food with glad and generous hearts, praising God and having the goodwill of all the people. And day by day the Lord added to their number those who were being saved.

Reflections through the Word

1. The Church begins

    a. Why did Luke write the Book of Acts? *(The Book of Acts is generally viewed as an extension to Luke's gospel).*

    - <u>Luke 1:3-4</u> I too decided, after investigating everything carefully from the very first, to write an orderly account for you, most excellent Theophilus, so that you may know the truth concerning the things about which you have been instructed.

    b. What purpose does the Book of Acts serve for the believer today?

2. The community

    a. Think about why God wanted the church to be among a community of believers.

DAY IV - Give Me a Clean Heart

3. The Word

   a. In reference to the focal passage what does "devoted" mean? What does it mean to you?

      1) What words come to mind when you look at this scripture?
      2) <u>Psalm 133:1</u> How very good and pleasant it is when kindred live together in unity!
      3) <u>John 17:23</u> I in them and you in me, that they may become completely one, so that the world may know that you have sent me and have loved them even as you have loved me.
      4) <u>1 Corinthians 1:10</u> Now I appeal to you, brothers and sisters, by the name of our Lord Jesus Christ, that all of you be in agreement and that there be no divisions among you, but that you be united in the same mind and the same purpose.
      5) <u>Ephesians 4:1-3</u> I, therefore, the prisoner in the Lord, beg you to lead a life worthy of the calling to which you have been called, with all humility and gentleness, with patience, bearing with one another in love, making every effort to maintain the unity of the Spirit in the bond of peace.

Saint Cyprian of Carthage believed Luke was referencing the "common mind [that] prevailed once, at the time of the Apostles," as this "common mind" was documented in the opening chapters of Acts, "God is one, and Christ is one, and His Church is one; one is the faith, and one the people cemented together by harmony into the strong unity of a body."[245]

> b. What scripture in the Bible comes to mind when you see this discipline?
>
>> 1) 2 Timothy 3:16-17 All scripture is inspired by God and is useful for teaching, for reproof, for correction, and for training in righteousness, so that everyone who belongs to God may be proficient, equipped for every good work.
>> 2) Psalm 119:11 I treasure your word in my heart, so that I may not sin against you.
>> 3) 2 Timothy 2:15 Do your best to present yourself to God as one approved by him, a worker who has no need to be ashamed, rightly explaining the word of truth.
>> 4) Joshua 1:8 This book of the law shall not depart out of your mouth; you shall meditate on it day and night, so that you may

---

[245] Jaroslav Pelikan, *Brazos Theological Commentary of the Bible: Acts* (Grand Rapids, IL: Brazo Press, 2005), 58.

DAY IV - Give Me a Clean Heart

> be careful to act in accordance with all that is written in it. For then you shall make your way prosperous, and then you shall be successful.
>
> 5) Romans 12:2 Do not be conformed to this world, but be transformed by the renewing of your minds, so that you may discern what is the will of God—what is good and acceptable and perfect.
>
> 6) John 6:63 It is the spirit that gives life; the flesh is useless. The words that I have spoken to you are spirit and life.

The great theologian Martin Luther said, "It is not many books or much reading that makes men learned: but it is good things, however little of them, often read, that make me learned in the Scriptures and make them godly, too. Indeed the writing of all the holy fathers should be read only for a time, in order that through them we may be led to the Holy Scriptures. We are like men who study the signposts and never travel the road. The dear fathers wished, by their writings, to lead us to the Scriptures, though the Scriptures alone are our vineyard in which we all ought to work and toil."[246]

---

[246] Mel Lawrenz, *The Dynamics of Spiritual Formation* (Grand Rapids, MI: Baker Books, 2000), 59.

It's About Relationships

Notes

DAY IV - Give Me a Clean Heart

Questions to Ponder

- What is the author's description of the early church in our focal passage?
- What spiritual disciplines do we find in our focal passage?
- What is the first discipline you see?
- In your opinion, what is Martin Luther's statement saying to us?
- We have indicated in previous sessions that the Bible has helped us through reconciliation. How has the Bible helped you?
- What are some ways you stay devoted to the apostles' teaching?

Application

How will you apply what you have learned today?

1.

2.

3.

Closing Prayer

Lord... [Spend time in prayer asking God to forgive you and help you to forgive others.]

Thank God in advance. Amen.

DAY V - Bind Us Together - Fellowship

Bing Us Together, Lord, Bind us together
With cords that cannot be broken.
Bind us together, Lord,
Bind us together,
Bind us together with love.

There is only one God,
There is only one King;
there is only one Body,
That is why we sing:[247]

Scripture Reading

Acts 2:42-47

They devoted themselves to the apostles' teaching and fellowship, to the breaking of bread and the prayers. Awe came upon everyone, because many wonders and signs were being done by the apostles. All who believed were

---

[247] Gospel Music Lyrics, *Bind Us Together*, https://gospelyrics.blogspot.com/2007/09/bind-us-together.html (accessed May 9, 2014).

together and had all things in common; they would sell their possessions and goods and distribute the proceeds to all, as any had need. Day by day, as they spent much time together in the temple, they broke bread at home and ate their food with glad and generous hearts, praising God and having the goodwill of all the people. And day by day the Lord added to their number those who were being saved.

Reflection through the Word

1) Fellowship

    a. What is the next discipline we see in this passage?
    b. Define "fellowship."

        i. Review the following passages on fellowship and, in your own words, discuss what they mean.

            1. <u>1 Corinthians 1:9</u> God is faithful; by him you were called into the fellowship of his Son, Jesus Christ our Lord.
            2. <u>Galatians 2:9</u> And when James and Cephas and John, who were acknowledged pillars, recognized the grace that had been given to me, they gave to Barnabas and me the right hand of

fellowship, agreeing that we should go to the Gentiles and they to the circumcised.

3. <u>Philippians 3:10</u> I want to know Christ and the power of his resurrection and the sharing of his sufferings by becoming like him in his death.

2) Koinonia as fellowship

   a. What do you know about Koinonia?

Malina states that fellowship may mean spending time together as in a social club. However, given the fact that group members did pool their resources, the word would mean that Luke is referring to the mutual obligations of partnership or association between one person and one or more other people with regard to a particular action, thing or person. It is a type of informal partnership contract. Partners were obligated to support the project of the group from their resources.[248]

---

[248] Bruce J. Malina, *Social Science Commentary on the Book of Acts* (Minneapolis, MN: Fortress Press, 2008), 36.

3) Koinonia as communion

   a. Define "communion."
   b. Review the following passages on communion and, in your own words, discuss what they mean.

      i. <u>Acts 2:42</u> They devoted themselves to the apostles' teaching and fellowship, to the breaking of bread and the prayers.
      ii. <u>1 Corinthians 10:16-17</u> The cup of blessing that we bless, is it not a sharing in the blood of Christ? The bread that we break, is it not a sharing in the body of Christ?
      iii. <u>1 John 1:1-7</u> We declare to you what was from the beginning, what we have heard, what we have seen with our eyes, what we have looked at and touched with our hands, concerning the word of life— this life was revealed, and we have seen it and testify to it, and declare to you the eternal life that was with the Father and was revealed to us— we declare to you what we have seen and heard so that you also may have fellowship with us; and truly our fellowship is with the Father and with his Son Jesus Christ. We are writing these things so that our joy may be complete. God Is Light. This is the

DAY V - Bind Us Together - Fellowship

> message we have heard from him and proclaim to you, that God is light and in him there is no darkness at all. If we say that we have fellowship with him while we are walking in darkness, we lie and do not do what is true; but if we walk in the light as he himself is in the light, we have fellowship with one another, and the blood of Jesus his Son cleanses us from all sin.

4) Koinonia as sharing

   a. Review the passages on sharing and, in your own words, discuss what they mean.

      i. <u>Romans 15:26</u> For Macedonia and Achaia have been pleased to share their resources with the poor among the saints at Jerusalem.
      ii. <u>1 Corinthians 10:16</u> The cup of blessing that we bless, is it not a sharing in the blood of Christ? The bread that we break, is it not a sharing in the body of Christ?
      iii. <u>2 Corinthians 8:3-4</u> For, as I can testify, they voluntarily gave according to their means, and even beyond their means, begging us earnestly for the privilege of sharing in this ministry to the saints.

iv. <u>Hebrews 13:16</u> Do not neglect to do good and to share what you have, for such sacrifices are pleasing to God.

5) Koinonia and breaking bread

   a. What kind of atmosphere can dining together create?

As indicated previously, Luke mentions breaking of bread twice: "here possibly a distinction between a regular meal (partook of food) and Eucharistic rite (breaking of bread) is suggested, even though originally both were integrated into one event."[249]

Application

How will you apply what you have learned today?

1.

2.

3.

---

[249] "The Breaking of Bread," *The Anchor Bible Dictionary,* Vol 4, ed. David Noel Freedman (New York, NY: Doubleday, 1992), 366.

DAY V - Bind Us Together - Fellowship

Closing Prayer

Lord... [Spend time in prayer asking God to bind us together in brotherly love.]

Thank God in advance. Amen.

DAY VI - I Need Thee - Prayer

I need Thee every hour, most gracious Lord;
No tender voice like Thine can peace afford.

Refrain:
I need Thee, oh, I need Thee;
Every hour I need Thee;
Oh, bless me now, my Savior,
I come to Thee.

I need Thee every hour, stay Thou nearby;
Temptations lose their power when Thou art nigh.

I need Thee every hour, in joy or pain;
Come quickly and abide, or life is vain.

I need Thee every hour; teach me Thy will;
and Thy rich promises in me fulfill.

I need Thee every hour, most Holy One;
Oh, make me Thine indeed, Thou blessed Son.[250]

---

[250] The Hymn Site, *I Need Thee Every Hour*, http://www.hymnsite.com/lyrics/umh397.sht (accessed May 9, 2014).

Scripture Reading

<u>Acts 2:42-47</u>

> They devoted themselves to the apostles' teaching and fellowship, to the breaking of bread and the prayers. Awe came upon everyone, because many wonders and signs were being done by the apostles. All who believed were together and had all things in common; they would sell their possessions and goods and distribute the proceeds to all, as any had need. Day by day, as they spent much time together in the temple, they broke bread at home and ate their food with glad and generous hearts, praising God and having the goodwill of all the people. And day by day the Lord added to their number those who were being saved.

Reflections through the Word

1. Prayer

    a. What scriptures on prayer do you keep dear to your heart?

    1) <u>1 Chronicles 16:11</u> Seek the LORD and his strength, seek his presence continually.

DAY V - Bind Us Together - Fellowship

2) <u>Proverbs 15:29</u> The LORD is far from the wicked, but he hears the prayer of the righteous.
3) <u>Matthew 7:11</u> If you then, who are evil, know how to give good gifts to your children, how much more will your Father in heaven give good things to those who ask him!
4) <u>Romans 8:26</u> Likewise the Spirit helps us in our weakness; for we do not know how to pray as we ought, but that very Spirit intercedes with sighs too deep for words.
5) <u>Philippians 4:6</u> Do not worry about anything, but in everything by prayer and supplication with thanksgiving let your requests be made known to God.
6) <u>Colossians 4:2</u> Devote yourselves to prayer, keeping alert in it with thanksgiving.
7) <u>1 Thessalonians 5:17</u> Pray without ceasing.
8) <u>1 Timothy 2:8</u> I desire, then, that in every place the men should pray, lifting up holy hands without anger or argument.
9) <u>James 1:7</u> for the doubter, being double-minded and unstable in every way, must not expect to receive anything from the Lord.

10) James 4:3 You ask and do not receive, because you ask wrongly, in order to spend what you get on your pleasures.
11) James 5:16 Therefore confess your sins to one another, and pray for one another, so that you may be healed. The prayer of the righteous is powerful and effective.
12) 1 John 1:9 If we confess our sins, he who is faithful and just will forgive us our sins and cleanse us from all unrighteousness.

2. Prayer and God

   a. 1 Samuel 1:9-11 After they had eaten and drunk at Shiloh, Hannah rose and presented herself before the LORD. Now Eli the priest was sitting on the seat beside the doorpost of the temple of the LORD. She was deeply distressed and prayed to the LORD, and wept bitterly. She made this vow: "O LORD of hosts, if only you will look on the misery of your servant, and remember me, and not forget your servant, but will give to your servant a male child, then I will set him before you as a nazirite until the day of his death. He shall drink neither wine nor intoxicants, and no razor shall touch his head."
   b. Daniel 9:3-6 Then I turned to the Lord God, to seek an answer by prayer and supplication

DAY V - Bind Us Together - Fellowship

with fasting and sackcloth and ashes. I prayed to the LORD my God and made confession, saying, "Ah, Lord, great and awesome God, keeping covenant and steadfast love with those who love you and keep your commandments, we have sinned and done wrong, acted wickedly and rebelled, turning aside from your commandments and ordinances. We have not listened to your servants the prophets, who spoke in your name to our kings, our princes, and our ancestors, and to all the people of the land.

c. <u>2 Chronicles 20:5-12</u> Jehoshaphat stood in the assembly of Judah and Jerusalem, in the house of the LORD, before the new court, and said, "O LORD, God of our ancestors, are you not God in heaven? Do you not rule over all the kingdoms of the nations? In your hand are power and might, so that no one is able to withstand you. Did you not, O our God, drive out the inhabitants of this land before your people Israel, and give it forever to the descendants of your friend Abraham? They have lived in it, and in it have built you a sanctuary for your name, saying, 'If disaster comes upon us, the sword, judgment, or pestilence, or famine, we will stand before this house, and before you, for your name is in this house, and cry to you in our distress, and you will hear and save.' See

> now, the people of Ammon, Moab, and Mount Seir, whom you would not let Israel invade when they came from the land of Egypt, and whom they avoided and did not destroy— they reward us by coming to drive us out of your possession that you have given us to inherit. O our God, will you not execute judgment upon them? For we are powerless against this great multitude that is coming against us. We do not know what to do, but our eyes are on you."

"Just as Luke has set up in Luke-Acts the parallelism between the Spirit's work in relation to Jesus and the Spirit's work in the church, so he also sets up the parallelism between prayer in the life of Jesus and prayer in the life of the Church."[251]

3. Prayer and Jesus

   a. What does the Bible say about Jesus and prayer?

   1) <u>Luke 6:12</u> Now during those days he went out to the mountain to pray; and he spent the night in prayer to God.

---

[251] Longnecker, 290.

DAY V - Bind Us Together - Fellowship

2) <u>Luke 18:1</u> Then Jesus told them a parable about their need to pray always and not to lose heart.
3) <u>Matthew 6:9-13</u> Pray then in this way: Our Father in heaven, hallowed be your name. Your kingdom come. Your will be done, on earth as it is in heaven. Give us this day our daily bread. And forgive us our debts, as we also have forgiven our debtors. And do not bring us to the time of trial, but rescue us from the evil one.

4. Prayer of Praise

    a. Look at Acts 2:42 and Acts 2:47.

        i. Praise - <u>Psalm 150</u> Praise the LORD! Praise God in his sanctuary; praise him in his mighty firmament! Praise him for his mighty deeds; praise him according to his surpassing greatness! Praise him with trumpet sound; praise him with lute and harp! Praise him with tambourine and dance; praise him with strings and pipe! Praise him with clanging cymbals; praise him with loud clashing cymbals! Let everything that breathes praise the LORD!
        ii. Thanksgiving - <u>Psalm 103:1-5</u> Bless the LORD, O my soul, and all that is within me, bless his holy name. Bless the LORD, O my

> soul, and do not forget all his benefits—who forgives all your iniquity, who heals all your diseases, who redeems your life from the Pit, who crowns you with steadfast love and mercy, who satisfies you with good as long as you live so that your youth is renewed like the eagle's.

Parsons explains that prayer has a vertical dimension in the community praising God, and a horizontal dimension in prayer directed outward to all the people.[252]

Questions to Ponder

- What is prayer? What does it mean to you?
- What do the above scriptures tell us about praying to God?

Application

How will you apply what you have learned today?

1.
2.
3.

---

[252] Parsons, 49.

DAY V - Bind Us Together - Fellowship

Closing Prayer

Lord... [Spend time in prayer asking God to draw you near.]

Thank God in advance. Amen.

Chapter Four

Summing It All Up

> No one is immune from relationship problems, which often build walls of indifference, anger, and nonchalant attitudes toward family members, friends, and especially the community of faith. Education and practice lead to changes in the amount of knowledge people have, in skills and competencies, in the way we communicate and understand each other, in our sense of self, and in the social world.[253]

THE HOPE IS that this book will spotlight the need for reconciliation among believers. The pain and disconnections are deeper than we can imagine. Many people have the freedom that is only found in Christ. They have gained

---

[253] Patricia Cranton, *Professional Development as Transformative Learning: New Perspectives for Teachers of Adults* (San Francisco, CA: The Jossey-Bass Publishers, 1996), 160.

the Kingdom of God and accepted the love of God, but are having a difficult time relating to and forgiving family members on a day-to-day basis. If we look around, we see evidence of families hurting and disconnected due to various conflicts.

After reading this book and applying the six study sessions, we should be able to openly discuss hurt, or the reasons why we have failed to reconcile specific situations in our lives. We will have greater insight on the magnitude of our hurt, and recognize that we are not alone. May we unite in community and lean on God's design of community as our support system. We are all in this together. Therefore, let us confidently open our hearts to receive the Word through the application of the disciplines identified.

Dr. Dorothea Johnson James

"Whoever believes in Him will not be disappointed."
Romans 10:11

Background: A native of Queens, New York, Dr. Dorothea James was raised in Baltimore, Maryland. Her journey has been a testament to faith, dedication, and a commitment to service in various capacities.

Educational Achievements: Dr. James values lifelong learning and holds the following degrees:

- Bachelor of Science in Psychology from Washington Bible College, Lanham, MD
- Master of Religion and Master of Divinity degrees from Liberty Theological Seminary, Lynchburg, VA
- Doctorate in Ministry from United Theological Seminary, Dayton, Ohio
- Board Certified Clinical Chaplain and Pastoral Counselor

Published Works and Webinars: Dr. James is the author of *All the King's Horses and All the King's Men: Reconciling*

Relationships through Spiritual Disciplines and a contributor to *I Need A Word: Sermons For Special Seasons*, Vol.1 by Dr. Vernon D. Shelton Sr. She has also facilitated several webinars, including "Why African Americans Do Not Choose Hospice" and "Disenfranchised Grief and Diversity."

Ministry and Mentorship: Dr. James is known for effectively encouraging, exhorting, mentoring, and making disciples through workshops, one-on-one counseling sessions, seminars, teaching, and preaching opportunities. Her unique ability to infuse humor and hope into her message resonates with her audience.

Personal Life: Beyond her professional achievements, Dr. James considers herself a practical theologian, emphasizing the importance of reconciling relationships. She is a motivational speaker, nouthetic counselor, preacher, and teacher. Dr. James is the devoted wife of Lawrence Timothy James Jr., a loving mother to one daughter, La'Don S. Marie [Adam James Johnson], and a godson, Sean Thompson Jr. She is a proud grandmother to Ajaiyla Joy and Autumn Murie.

Inspiration and Testimony: Her guiding scripture is 1 Corinthians 10:13: "No temptation has overtaken you but such as is common to man; and God is faithful, who will not allow you to be tempted beyond what you are able, but with the temptation will provide the way of escape also, so that you will be able to endure it." In the face of trials, her testimony is "It is Well with My Soul," believing that failure does not mark the end but a chance for a new beginning.

A Spiritual Discipline is an intentionally directed action which places us in a position to receive from God the power to do what we cannot accomplish on our own.

–Richard Foster

Bibliography

Affleck, Bert. "John Wesley's Spiritual Disciplines for Today's Pastor," *Perkins Journal* 40, no.1. (January 1987).

Ammerman, Nancy T. and others. *Studying Congregations: A New Handbook.* Nashville, TN: Abingdon Press, 1998.

Armstrong, John, and others. *A Servant's Journal, 21 Articles on Reconciliation, Fellowship & The Grace of God.* Vol. 2. New Lennox, IL: Leadership Resource International, 1992.

Anderson, Neil. *Victory over the Darkness.* Ventura, CA: Regal Books, 1990.

Anderson, Ray S. *The Shape of Practical Theology: Empowering Ministry with Theological Praxis.* Downers Grove, IL: IVP Academic, 2001.

Andrew, Dale P. *Practical Theology for Black Churches: Bringing Black Theology and African-American Folk Religion.* Louisville, KY: Westminster John Knox Press, 2002.

Alexander, Claude. *Necessary Christianity: Living a Must Life, in a Maybe World.* Chicago, IL: MMGI Books, 2013.

Allen, Michael J. & James B. Allen. *World History From 1500.* New York, NY: Harper Collins Publisher, 1993.

Alsup, John. "Prayer, Consciousness, and the Early Church: a Look at Acts 2:41-47 for Today," *Austin Seminary Bulletin* 4, no. 101 (1985).

Anglin, Jay Pascal & William J. Hamblin. *World History to 1648.* New York, NY: Harper Collins Publisher, 1993.

Baldwin, Joyce G. *The Message of Genesis 12-50: from Abraham to Joseph.* Leicester, England: IVP Academic, 1986.

Barna, George. *Growing True Disciples.* Colorado Springs, CO: Water Brook Press, 2001.

Balswick, Jack and Judith. *The Family: A Christian Perspective on the Contemporary Home.* Grand Rapids, MI: Baker Publishing Group, 2007.

Beasley-Topliffe, Keith, ed. *The Upper Room Dictionary of Christian Spiritual Formation.* Nashville: Upper Room Books, 2003.

Benner, David and Peter C. Hill, ed. *Baker Encyclopedia of Psychology and Counseling, Baker Reference Library.* Grand Rapids, MI: Baker Books, 1999.

Bettenson, Henry and Chris Maunder eds. *Documents of the Christian Church,* 2nd ed. New York, NY: Oxford University Press, 1963.

Blenkinsopp, Joseph and John Challenor. *Scripture Discussion, Commentary: Pentateuch.* Chicago, IL: ACTA Foundation, 1971.

Bibliography

Bloesch, Donald G. *The Struggle of Prayer.* San Francisco, CA: Harper & Row Publishers, 1980.

Blount, Brian K., Cain Hope Felder, Clarice J. Martin, and Emerson B. Powery, eds. *True to Our Native Land: An African American New Testament Commentary.* Minneapolis, MN: Fortress Press, 2007.

Bonhoeffer, Dietrich. *Life Together: The Classic Exploration of Faith in Community.* New York: Harper & Row, Publishers, 1954.

———. *The Cost of Discipleship.* Nashville, TN: Broadman & Holman Publishers, 1998.

Bouyer, Louis, ed. *Dictionary of Theology.* Tournai: Desclee & Co., 1963.

Bright, John. *A History of Israel.* 4th ed. Louisville, KY: Westminster John Knox Press, 2000.

Brodie, Thomas L. *Genesis as Dialogue: A Literary, Historical, and Theological Commentary.* New York: Oxford University Press, 2001.

Browning, Don S. *A Fundamental Practical Theology: Descriptive and Strategic Proposals.* Minneapolis: Fortress Press, 1996.

———. "Toward a Practical Theology of Care." *Union Seminary Quarterly Review* 36, no. 2-3 (Winter 1981).

Browning, Robert L., and Roy A. Reed. *Forgiveness, Reconciliation, and Moral Courage: Motives and Designs for*

Ministry in a Troubled World. Grand Rapids, MI: Eerdmans Publishing Company, 2004.

Brueggemann, Walter. *Genesis: Interpretation, a Bible Commentary For Teaching and Preaching*. Atlanta, GA: Knox Press, 1982.

Brueggemann, Walter, and Tod Linafelt. *An Introduction to the Old Testament, Second Edition: the Canon and Christian Imagination (canon and Christian Imagination)*. 2 ed. Louisville, KY: Westminster John Knox Press, 2012.

Brueggemann, Walter and James May, ed. etc. *Genesis: Interpretation: A Bible Commentary for Teaching and Preaching*. Atlanta: Knox Press, 1982.

Bruce, F. F. *The Book of Acts Revised Edition*. Grand Rapids, MI: William B. Eerdmans Publishing Company, 1988.

Campbell, Alastair. *The Blackwell Reader in Pastoral and Practical Theology*, eds. James Woodward and Stephen Pattison. Malden, MA: Blackwell Publishers, 2000.

Campolo, Tony, and Michael Battle. *The Church Enslaved: a Spirituality of Racial Reconciliation*. Minneapolis, MN: Augsburg Books, 2005.

Calhoun, Adele Ahlberg. *Spiritual Disciplines Handbook: Practices That Transform Us*. Downers Grove, IL: Inter Varsity Press Books, 2005.

Cairns, Earle E. *Christianity Through the Centuries: A History of the Christian Church* Grand Rapids, MI: Zondervan Publishing House, 1996.

Calian, Carnegie Samuel. "Christian Faith as Forgiveness." *Theology Today* 37, no. 4 (1981): 439-443. *ATLA Religion Database with ATLASerials*, EBSCO*host* (accessed February 6, 2014).

Clarke, Andrew, and Bruce Winter, eds. *The Book of Acts in Its Ancient Literary Setting*. Grand Rapids, MI: Paternoster, 1994.

Coats, George W. "Redactional unity in Genesis 37-50." *Journal Of Biblical Literature* 93, no. 1 (March 1, 1974): 15-21. *ATLA Religion Database with ATLASerials*, EBSCO*host* (accessed March 18, 2012).

Coates, Thomas. "Fellowship." *Concordia Theological Monthly* 39, no. 3 (1968): 52-63.

Cole, Neil. *Organic Church: Growing Faith Where Life Happens*. San Francisco, CA: Jossey-Bass, 2005.

Collins, Gary R. *The Biblical Basis of Christian Counseling for People Helpers: Relating the Basic Teachings of Scripture to People's Problems.* Colorado Springs, CO: NavPress Publishing, 1993.

Cone, James H., and Gayraud S. Wilmore, eds. *Black Theology: A Documentary History 1980-1992.* Vol I. Maryknoll: Orbis Books, 1993.

Cone, James H. *The Cross and the Lynching Tree*. Maryknoll, NY: Orbis Books, 2011

Crabb, Larry. *Connecting: Healing for Ourselves and Our Relationships a Radical New Vision*. Nashville, TN: Word Publishing, 1997.

Cairns, Earle E. *Christianity through the Centuries: A History of the Christian Church*. 3rd ed. Grand Rapids, MI: Zondervan Publishing House, 1996.

Cranton, Patricia. *Professional Development as Transformative Learning: New Perspective of Teachers of Adults*. San Francisco: Jossey-Bass, 1996.

Creswell, John W. *Research Design: Qualitative, Quantitative, and Mixed Methods Approaches*. 3rd ed. Sage, Thousand Oaks, 2009.

Crouch Jr., William H. and Joel C. Gregory. *What We Love About the Black Church: Can We Get a Witness?* Valley Forge, PA: Judson Press, 2010.

Dallen, James. *The Reconciling Community: The Rite of Penance*. New York, NY: Pueblo Publishing Company, 1986.

Dalton, Lucius M. *The Lord Will Provide*. Bloomington, IL: Author House, 2011.

Daniel, Eleanor, John Wade, and Charles Gresham, *Introduction to Christian Education*. Cincinnati, OH: Standard Publishing Company, 1997.

Dawn, Marva J. *Reaching Out Without Dumbing Down: a Theology of Worship for the Turn-of-the-century Culture*. Grand Rapids, MI: Wm. B. Eerdmans Publishing Company, 1995.

_____. *Talking the Walk: Letting Christian Language Live Again*. Grand Rapids: MI: Brazos Press, 2005.

_____. *Truly the Community: Romans 12 and How to Be the Church*. Grand Rapids, MI: William B. Eerdmans Publishing Company, 1992.

Dawn, Marva and Eugene Peterson. *The Unnecessary Pastor: Rediscovering the Call*. Grand Rapids, MI: William B. Eerdmans Publishing Company, 2000.

Dever, Mark. *The Church: The Gospel Made Visible*. Nashville, TN: B & H Academic, 2012.

Dillard, Raymond B. and Tremper Longman III, *An Introduction to the Old Testament* Grand Rapids, MI: Zondervan, 1994.

Douglas, J. D. "Grudge," eds. D. R. W. Wood et al., *New Bible Dictionary*. Downers Grove, IL: Intervarsity Press, 1996.

Eckerman, James P. *Exploring Church History*. Wheaton, IL: Crossway Books, 2002.

Eleanor Daniel, John Wade, and Charles Gresham. *Introduction to Christian Education*. Cincinnati, OH: Standard Publishing, 1980.

Eliot, T. S. "Choruses from The Rock," *Complete Poems and Plays*. New York, NY: Harcourt & Brace, 1952.

Elmore, John Hull & Tim. *Pivotal Praying: Connecting with God in Times of Great Need*. Nashville, TN: Thomas Nelson, 2002.

Elwell, W. A., ed. *Baker Encyclopedia of the Bible*. Grand Rapids, MI: Baker Book House, 1998.

Elwell, W. A. and B. J. Beitzel. eds. *Baker Encyclopedia of the Bible*. Grand Rapids, MI: Baker Book House, 1998.

Elwell, W. A. and P. W. Comfort eds., *Tyndale Bible Dictionary*. Wheaton, IL: Tyndale House Publishers, 2001.

Encyclopedia Britannica from Encyclopedia Britannica Online. Available from http://www.britannica.com.

Encyclopedia Dictionary of the Bible. New York: McGraw-Hill Book Company, 1963.

Encyclopedic Dictionary of the Bible, Louis F. Hartman, ed. and trans. New York, NY: McGraw-Hill Book Company, 1963.

Erickson, Millard. *Introducing Christian Doctrine*. Grand Rapids, IL: Baker Book House, 1992.

Fee, Gordon D., and Robert L. Jr. Hubbard, eds. *The Eerdmans Companion to the Bible*. Grand Rapids, MI: Wm. B. Eerdmans Publishing Company, 2011.

Bibliography

Fiensy, David. *The College Press NIV Commentary New Testament* Introduction. Joplin, MO: College Press Publishing, 1994.

Flanigan, Beverly. *Forgiving the Unforgivable: Overcoming the Bitter Legacy of Intimate Wounds.* New York, NY: Collier Books, 1992.

Foster, Richard J. *Celebration of Discipline: the Path to Spiritual Growth.* 20th ed. San Francisco: Harper San Francisco, 1998.

Fowler, James W. "Practical Theology and Theological Education: Some Models and Questions." *Theology Today* 42, no. (1 April 1985).

Freedman, David Noel, Allen C. Myers, and Astrid B. Beck, eds *Eerdmans Dictionary of the Bible.* Grand Rapids, MI: Eerdmans Pub Co, 2000.

Fretheim, Terrance L. *"Genesis."* In *The New Interpreter's Bible,* Vol I. ed. David L. Peterson. Nashville, TN: Abingdon Press, 1994.

Fritsch, Charles T. "God was with him" : a theological study of the Joseph narrative." *Interpretation* 9, no. 1 (January 1, 1955): 21-34. *ATLA Religion Database with ATLASerials,* EBSCO*host* (accessed February 21, 2012).

Gaventa, Beverly R. *Abingdon New Testament Commentaries: Acts.* Nashville, TN: Abingdon Press, 2003.

Geiger, Eric, Michael Kelley & Philip Nation. *Transformational Discipleship: How People Really Grow*. Nashville, TN: B & H Publishing Group, 2012.

Gonzales, Justo L. *Acts: The Gospel of the Spirit*. New York, NY: Orbis Books, 2001.

_____. *The Story of Christianity: The Early Church to the Dawn of the Reformation*. Vol 1. New York, NY: Harper Collins Publishers, 1984.

_____. *The Story of Christianity: The Reformation to the Present Day*. Vol 2. New York, NY: Harper Collins Publishers, 1985.

Gorman, Michael J. *Apostle of the Crucified Lord: A Theological Introduction to Paul & His Letters*. Grand Rapids, MI: William B. Eerdmans Publishing Company, 2004.

Graham, Elaine. *The Blackwell Reader in Pastoral and Practical Theology*, eds. James Woodward and Stephen Pattison. Malden, MA: Blackwell Publishers, 2000.

Graves Jr., Lorenzo. "From Egypt to Canaan Land 1500 to 1400 B.C.: A Comparative Experience of the Growth of the Calvary Baptist Church 1958 to 1978 A.D." Master's Thesis, United Baptist College and Seminary, 1978.

Greenwood, Davydd J. and Morten Levin. *Introduction to Action Research: Social Research for Social Change*. Thousand Oaks, CA: SAGE Publications Inc., 2nd ed. 2007.

Greidanus, Sidney. *Preaching Christ From Genesis*. Grand Rapids, MI: William B. Eerdmans Publishing, 2007.

Griffin, Emory. *Getting Together: A Guide for Good Groups*. Downers Grove, IL: IVP Academic, 1982.

Grigsby, Victor J. *The Guide for Building Godly Homes: Family Matters*. New Brighton, PA: Penn Eagle Publishing, 2010.

Hanson, Paul D. *The People Called: The Growth of Community in the Bible*. San Francisco, CA: Harper & Row Publisher, 1986.

Harris, James H. *Pastoral Theology: A Black-Church Perspective*. Minneapolis: Fortress Press, 1991.

Herrington, Jim, Mike Bonem and James H. Furr. *Leading Congregational Change: A Practical Guide for the Transformational Journey*. San Francisco, CA: Jossey-Bass Publishers, 2000.

Heath, Gordon L. *Doing Church History*. Toronto: Clements Publishing, 2008.

Hellwig, Monika K. *Sign of Reconciliation and Conversion: The Sacrament of Penance for Our Times*. Wilmington, DE: Michael Glazier, Inc.

Hess, Lisa M. *Artisanal Theology: Intentional Formation in Radically Covenantal Companionship*. Eugene, OR: Wipf & Stock Pub, 2009.

Howe, Leroy T. "Beginnings in Practical Theology: An Account of a Journey," *Perkins Journal* 35, no. 3. (Summer

1982). ALTA Religion Database with ATLASerials EBSCO Host (accessed December 12, 2012).

Huges, Kent & Barbara Huges. *Disciplines of a Godly Family*. Wheaton, IL: Crossway Books, 1995.

Humphreys, W. Lee. *The Character of God in the Book of Genesis*. Louisville, KY: John Knox Press, 2001.

Icenogle, Gareth Weldon. *Biblical Foundations for Small Group Ministry: An Integrative Approach*. Downers Grove, IL: Intervarsity Press, 1993. under chap. 1, sec. "God's Call To Small Group Community." Logos Bible Software.

Jeffress, Robert *When Forgiveness Doesn't Make Sense*. Colorado Springs, CO: WaterBrook Press, 2008.

Jenkins, Willis and Jennifer M. McBride. eds. *Bonhoeffer and King: Their Legacies and Import for Christian and Social Thought*. Minneapolis, MN: Fortress Press, 2010.

Johnson, Susanne *Christian Spiritual Formation in the Church and Classroom*. Nashville, TN: Abingdon Press, 1989.

Johnson, Victoria. *Restoring Broken Vessels: Confronting the Attack of Female Sexuality*. Detroit, MI: Dabar Publishing Company, 1995.

Jones, Gregory L. *Embodying Forgiveness: A Theological Analysis*. Grand Rapids, MI: William B. Eerdmans Publishing Company, 1995.

Kass, Leon R. *The Beginning of Wisdom: Reading Genesis*. Chicago, IL: The University of Chicago Press, 2003.

Kelly, Gregory B. Kelly and F. Burton Nelson. *The Cost of Moral Leadership*. Grand Rapid, MI: William B. Eerdmans Publishing Company, 2003.

King Jr., Martin Luther. *Where Do We Go From Here: Chaos or Community*. Boston, MA: Beacon Press, 1994.

Kornfeld, Margaret. *Cultivating Wholeness: a Guide to Care and Counseling in Faith Communities*. New York, NY: Bloomsbury Academic, 2000.

Kselman, John S. "Forgiveness" in *The Anchor Bible Dictionary*. Vol. 2, ed. David Noel Freedman. New York, NY: Doubleday, 1992.

Lane, George A. *Christian Spirituality: An Historical Sketch*. Chicago, IL: Loyola University Press, 1984.

Lawrenz, Mel. *The Dynamics of Spiritual Formation*. Grand Rapids, MI: Baker Books, 2000.

Lescher, Bruce, and Elizabeth Liebert, eds. *Exploring Christian Spirituality: Essays in Honor of Sandra M. Schneider*. Mahwah, NJ: Paulist Press, 2006.

Levinskaya, Irina. *The Book of Acts: In Its First Century Setting*. Vol 5. Grand Rapids, MI: William B. Eerdmans Publishing, 1996.

Lincoln, C. Eric, and Lawrence H. Mamiya. *The Black Church in the African-American Experience*. Durham, NC: Duke University Press Books, 1990.

Livingston, James C., Francis Schussler Fiorenza, with Sarah Coakley and James H. Evans, Jr. *Modern Christian Thought: The Twentieth Century*. Minneapolis, MN: 2006.

Longenecker, Richard N. *John and Acts*. Vol. 9. *The Expositor's Bible Commentary with New International Version*, ed. Frank E. Gaebelein, 205-573. Grand Rapids, MI: Zondervan, 1990.

Longman, Tremper, and III & Raymond B. Dillard. *An Introduction to the Old Testament*. 2nd ed. Grand Rapids, MI: Zondervan, 2006.

Lowery, Kevin Twain. "The Means of Grace: Wesley's Meditation between Naturalism and Mysticism" (2004) Faculty Scholarship Theology Paper 7. Available from http://www.digitalcommonsolivet.edu/theo_facp/7 (accessed January 21, 2014).

Lynch, Chuck. *I Should Forgive, But--: Finding Release from Anger and Bitterness*. Nashville, TN: Thomas Nelson, 1998.

Maas, Robin & Gabriel O'Donnell. *Spiritual Traditions for the Contemporary Church*. Nashville, TN: Abingdon Press, 1990.

Bibliography

Mack, Dr. Sir Walter. *How to Make a Wrong Relationship Right*. Tulsa, OK: Word and Spirit Resources, 2010.

Maddox, Robert. *Acts: The Laymen's Bible Book Commentary*. Vol. 19. Nashville, TN: Broadman Press, 1979.

Malina, Bruce J. *Social Science Commentary on the Book of Acts*. Minneapolis, MN: Fortress Press, 2008.

Mann, Thomas. *The Oxford Guide to Library Research*. 3rd ed. New York, NY: Oxford University Press, 2005.

Martin, Bernard. *The Healing Ministry in the Church*. Richard, VA: John Knox Press, 1960.

Massey, James Earl. *Spiritual Disciplines*. 3rd ed. Anderson, IN: Warner Press Inc., 1985.

Mathews, K. A. *The New American Commentary, Genesis 11:27-50:26*, vol. 1b. Nashville, TN: Broadman & Holman Publishers, 2005.

McClendon, Ruth & Leslie B. Kadis. *Reconciling Relationships and Preserving the Family Business: Tools for Success*. New York, NY: The Haworth Press, 2004.

McIntosh, Gary L. *One Size Doesn't Fit All: Bringing Out the Best in Any Size Church*. Grand Rapids, MI: Revell, 1999.

McMickle, Marvin A. *Caring Pastors, Caring People: Equipping Your Church for Pastoral Care (Living Church)*. Valley Forge, PA: Judson Pr, 2011.

McNiff, Jean, Pamela Lomax, and Jack Whitehead. *You and Your Action Research Project*. New York, NY: Routledge Farmer, 2003.

Meeks, Steve. *Relational Christianity: Experiencing Intimacy and Companionship With the Living God.* Houston TX: Calvary Publications, 1991.

Millgram, Hillel I. *The Joseph Paradox: Radical Reading of Genesis 37-50.* Jefferson, NC: McFarland & Company, Inc., 2012.

Mills, Robbie Edwards. *Church as the Surrogate Family.* Bloomington, IN: West Bow Press, 2011.

Mitchell, Henry H. *Black Church Beginnings: the Long-Hidden Realities of the First Years.* Grand Rapids, MI: Wm. B. Eerdmans Publishing Co., 2004.

Morgan, G. Campbell. *The Acts of the Apostles.* Old Tappan, NY: Fleming H. Revell Company, 1924.

Mulholland Jr., M. Robert. *Invitation to a Journey: A Road Map for Spiritual Formation.* Downers Grove, IL: Intervarsity Press, 1993.

Mursell, Gordon. *The Story of Christian Spirituality, Two Thousand Years from East to West.* Minneapolis, MN: Augsburg Fortress Press, 2001.

Musekura, L. Gregory Jones & Célestin. *Forgiving as We've Been Forgiven: Community Practices for Making Peace*. Downers Grove, IL: IVP Books, 2010.

Myers, A. C., ed. *Eerdmans Bible Dictionary*. Grand Rapids: William B. Eerdmans Publishing Company, 1987.

Myers, William R. *Research in Ministry: Primer for the Doctor of Ministry Program*. 3rd ed. Chicago, IL: Exploration Press, 2002.

Norman, Stan. "Redeem, Redemption, Redeemer," Edited by Chad Brand et al., *Holman Illustrated Bible Dictionary*. Nashville, TN: Holman Bible Publishers, 2003.

Okholm, Dennis L. [Editor]. *The Gospel in Black & White: Theological Resources for Racial Reconciliation*. Downers Grove, IL: Intervarsity Press, 1997.

Old, Hughes Oliphant. "Daily prayer in the Reformed Church of Strasburg, 1525-1530" *Worship 52*, no. (2 March 1978).

Osmer, Richard Robert. *Practical Theology: An Introduction*. Grand Rapids, MI: William B. Eerdmans Publishing, 2008.

Park, Andrew Sung. *From Hurt to Healing: a Theology of the Wounded*. Nashville, TN: Abingdon Press, 2004.

———. *The Wounded Heart of God: The Asian Concept of Han and the Christian Doctrine of Sin*.

Parson, Mikeal C. *Acts Paideia: Commentaries on the New Testament.* Grand Rapids: Baker Publishing Group, 2008.

Pennington, M Basil, Alan Jones, and Mark Booth. *The Living Testament: The Essential Writings of Christianity Since the Bible.* San Francisco: Harper & Row, 1985.

Pelikan, Jaroslav. *Brazos Theological Commentary of the Bible: Acts.* Grand Rapids, IL: Brazo Press, 2005.

Penzel, Klaus. "Some Thoughts on Schleiermacher and Practical Theology Today," *Perkins Journal* 35, no. 3 (Summer 1982).

Pleins, David. *The Social Visions of the Hebrew Bible: A Theological Introduction.* Louisville, KY: Westminster John Knox Press, 2001.

Pohly, Kenneth. *Transforming the Rough Places: The Ministry of Supervision.* 2nd ed. Franklin, TN: Providence House Publishers, 2011.

Poling, James N. & Donald E. Miller. *Foundations for a Practical Theology of Ministry.* Nashville, TN: Abingdon Press. 1985.
Powe, Jr. F. Douglas. *New Wine New Wineskins: How African American Congregations Can Reach New Generations.* Nashville, TN: Abingdon Press, 2012.

Proctor, Samuel DeWitt. *The Substance of Things Hoped for: A Memoir of African-American Faith.* New York: Valley Forge, PA: Judson Press, 1999.

Proctor, Samuel D. and Gardner C. Taylor. *We Have This Ministry: The Heart of the Pastor's Vocation.* Valley Forge, PA: Judson Press, 1996.

Rainer, Thom S., and Erick Geiger. *Simple Church: Returning to God's Process for Making Disciples.* Nashville, TN: B & H Publishing Group, 2011.

Robinson, Anthony B., and Robert Wall. *Called to Be Church.* Grand Rapids, MI: William B. Eerdmans, 2006.

Rogers, Donald B. *Urban Church Education.* Birmingham, AL: Religious Education Press, 1989.

Roley, Scott and James Isaac Elliott. *God's Neighborhood: A Hopeful Journey in Racial Reconciliation & Community Renewal.* Downers Grove, IL: Intervarsity Press, 2004.

Root, Andrew. "Practical Theology: What Is It and How Does it Work." *Journal of Youth Ministry* 7, no. 2 (May 2009).

Rowe, Hugh. *Joseph's Memoirs: Life Lessons for a Successful You.* Bloomington, IN: Author House, 2012.

Russell, Letty M. *Growth in Partnership.* Philadelphia, PA: The Westminster Press, 1981.

Ryrie, Charles. *Balancing the Christian Life.* Chicago, IL: The Moody Bible Institute, 1994.

_____. *Basic Theology: A Popular Systematic Guide to Understanding Biblical Truth.* Chicago, IL: Moody Press, 1986.

Sailhamer, John H. "Genesis," In *Genesis, Exodus, Leviticus, and Numbers*. Vol. 2. *The Expositor's Bible Commentary with the New International Version*, ed. Frank E. Gaebelein, 1-284. Grand Rapids, MI: Zondervan, 1990.

Salmeier, Michael A. *Restoring the Kingdom: The Role of God as the Ordainer of the Time and Seasons in the Acts of the Acts of the Apostles.* Eugene, OR: Pickwick Publications, 2001.

Seymour, Jack L. *Mapping Christian Education: Approaches to Congregational Learning.* Nashville, TN: Abingdon Press, 1997.

Seymour, Jack L. & Donald E. Miller. *Contemporary Approaches: Christian Education.* Nashville, TN: Abington Press, 1982.

Scaer, David P. "Luther on Prayer," *Concordia Theological Quarterly* 47, no. 4 (October 1983).

Schrier, Robert W. *Moral Courage, Abraham Lincoln, Mahatmas Gandhi, Nelson Mandela, and Martin Luther King Jr.* Lexington, KY: B&B Publishers, 2012.

Sinclair, Celcia. *Genesis.* Louisville, KY: Westminster Press, 1999.

Speiser, E. A., ed. *The Anchor Bible Dictionary*. Garden City: Doubleday, 1694.

Smith, Efrem. *The Post-Black & Post-White Church: Becoming the Beloved Community in a Multi-Ethnic World.* San Francisco, CA: Jossey-Bass, 2012.

Bibliography

Smith, James E. *The Pentateuch*. 2nd ed. Joplin, MO: College Press Publishing Company, Inc., 1996.

Stringfellow, William. *The Politics of Spirituality*. Philadelphia, PA: The Westminster Press, 1984.

Stone, Lance. "Forgiveness," *Journal for Preachers*, 29, no. 2 (2006): 46. *ATLA Religion Database with ATLASerials*, BSCO*host* (accessed March 21, 2012).

Strong, J. *Concise Dictionary of the Words in the Greek Testament and the Hebrew Bible*, vol. 2a. Bellingham, WA: Logos Bible Software, 2009.

Stuckwisch, Richard D. "Principles of Christian Prayer from the Third Century: A Brief Look at Origen, Tertullian and Cyprian With Some Comments on their Meaning Today," *Worship* 71, no.1 (January 1997).

Thatcher, Adrian. *Theology and Families*. Oxford, UK: Blackwell Pub., 2007.

Tidwell, Charles A. *The Educational Ministry of a Church: A Comprehensive Models for Students and Ministers*. Nashville, TN: Broadman & Holman Publishers, 1996.

Tiffany, Frederick C. and Sharon H. Ringe. *Biblical Interpretation: A Road Map*. Nashville, TN: Abingdon Press, 1996.

The Anchor Bible Dictionary. Vol. 2, ed. David Noel Freedman. New York, NY: Doubleday, 1992.

The Interpreter's Bible, Vol. IX, ed. George Arthur Buttrick. New York, NY: Abingdon Press, 1954.

The Interpreter's Dictionary of the Bible. Vol. 1 New York, NY: Abingdon Press, 1962.

The New Interpreter's Dictionary of the Bible. Vol. 4 Nashville, TN: Abington, 1976.

The New Interpreter's Bible: A Commentary in Twelve Volumes. Vol. 10, ed. Leander E. Keck et.al. Nashville, TN: Abingdon Press, 2002.

Thomas, Brodie. *Genesis a Dialogue: A Literary, Historical, and Theological Commentary*. New York, NY: Oxford Press.

Thomas, Owen C. and Ellen K. Wondra. *Introduction to Theology*. 3rd ed. Harrisburg, PA: Morehouse Publishing, 2002.

Thomas, R. L. *New American Standard Hebrew-Aramaic and Greek Dictionaries*. Anaheim, CA: Foundations Publications, Inc., 1998. Logos Bible Software.

Thompson, Andrew C. "John Wesley and the Means of Grace: Historical and Theological Context." ThD diss., Duke Divinity School, 2012.

Thurman, Howard. *Disciplines of the Spirit*. Richmond, IN: Friends United Press, 1963.

_____. *With Head and Heart: The Autobiography of Howard Thurman.* San Diego, CA: Harcourt Brace & Co., 1981.

Tutu, Desmond Mpilo. *No Future Without Forgiveness.* New York, NY: Doubleday, 1999.

Tye, Karen B. *Basics of Christian Education.* St. Louis, MO: Chalice Press, 2000.

Wall, Robert W., J. Paul Sampley, and N. T. Wright. *The New Interpreter's Bible: Acts—First Corinthians* vol. 10. Nashville, TN: Abingdon Press, 2002.

Walvood, John F., Roy B. Zuck, and Dallas Theological Seminary. *The Bible Knowledge Commentary: An Exposition of the Scriptures.* 2 Vols. Wheaton, IL: Victor Books, 1983.

Weaver, Andrew J. & Monica Furlong. *Reflections on Forgiveness and Spiritual Growth.* Nashville, TN: Abingdon Press, 2000.

Wenham, Gordon J. *Word Biblical Commentary: Genesis 1-15.* Vol 1. Waco, TX: Word Book Publisher, 1987.

Wenham, Gordon J., J. Alec Motyer, Donald A. Carson, and R. T. France, eds. *New Bible Commentary: 21st Century Edition.* 4th ed. Downers Grove, IL: IVP Academic, 1994.

Westerhoff, John H. *Inner Growth, Outer Change: An Educational Guide to Church Renewal.* New York, NY: Seabury Press, 1979.

Westerholm, Stephen "Forgiveness," *The New Interpreter's Dictionary of the Bible*. Vol. 2, ed. Katherine Doob Sakenfeld. Nashville, TN: Abingdon Press, 2007.

Westermann, Claus. *Genesis 37-50: A Continental Commentary*. Minneapolis, MN: Fortress Press, 2002.

Whelchel, L.H., and Jr. *The History and Heritage of African-American Churches: a Way Out of No Way*. St. Paul, MN: Paragon House, 2011.

Whitney, Donald S. *Spiritual Disciplines Within the Church: Participating Fully in the Body of Christ*. Chicago, IL: Moody Publishers, 1996.

_____. *Spiritual Disciplines For The Christian Life*. Colorado Springs, CO: Navpress, 1991.

Wielhouwer, Peter. "Impact of Church Activities and Socialization On African American Religious Commitment." *Social Science Quarterly* 3, no. 85 (2004): 767-92.

Wilhoit, James C. *Spiritual Formation as if the Church Mattered: Growing in Christ Through Community*. Grand Rapids, MI: Bakers Academic, 2008.

Wilkerson, Bruce and Kenneth Boa. *Talk Thru the Old Testament*. Nashville, TN: Thomas Nelson Publishers, 1983.

Willard, Dallas. *The Spirit of Disciplines: Understanding How God Changes Lives*. San Francisco, CA: Harper Collins Publishers, 1988.

Wink, Walter. *Engaging the Powers: Discernment and Resistance in a World of Domination*. Philadelphia, PA: Fortress Press, 1992.

_____. *When the Powers Fall: Reconciliation in the Healing of Nations*. Minneapolis, MN: Fortress Press, 1998.

Witherington III, Ben. *The Acts of the Apostles: a Socio-Rhetorical Commentary*. Grand Rapids, MI: Wm. B. Eerdmans Publishing Company, 1998.

Williams, P. J., Andrew Clarke, Peter Head, and David Instone-Brewer. *The New Testament in Its First Century Setting: Essays on Context and Background*. Grand Rapids, MI: William B. Eerdmans Publishing Company, 2004.

Wolfaardt, Johan A. "Practical Theology: Approaches to the Subject Called Practical Theology," *Journal of Theology for Southern Africa* no. 51 (June 1985).

Woodward, James, and Stephen Pattison. *The Blackwell Reader in Pastoral and Practical Theology*. Malden, MA: Blackwell Publishing, 2004.

Worthington Jr., Everett L. *Forgiving and Reconciling: Bridges to Wholeness and Hope*. Downers Grove, IL: InterVasity Press, 2003.

Vickers, Jason. *Mining the Good Ground: A Theology for Church Renewal*. Waco: Baylor University Press, 2011.

Vine, W. E., Merrill F. Unger, and William White Jr., "To Forgive" in *Vine's Complete Expository Dictionary of Old and New Testament Words*. Nashville: Thomas Nelson Publisher, 1984.

Von Rad, Gerhard. *Genesis,* rev. edition. Philadelphia, PA: The Westminster Press, 1972.

Vyhmeister, Nancy Jean. *Quality Research Papers for Students of Religion and Theology.* Grand Rapids, MI: Zondervan, 2008.

Printed in the USA
CPSIA information can be obtained
at www.ICGtesting.com
LVHW021510181024
794066LV00012B/364